RUN WITH THE BALL!

RUN WITH THE BALL!

A BRISK DASH THROUGH 150 YEARS OF RUGBY

DEREK ROBINSON

WILLOW BOOKS
Collins
8 Grafton Street, London W1
1984

Willow Books
William Collins Sons & Co Ltd
London · Glasgow · Sydney · Auckland
Toronto · Johannesburg

First published 1984
© Derek Robinson

British Library Cataloguing in Publication Data
Robinson, Derek
Run with the ball!
1. Rugby football—History
I. Title
796.33'3'09   GV944.85

ISBN 0 00 218077 4

Cartoons by Paul Davies

Set in Sabon
by Wyvern Typesetting Ltd, Bristol
Printed and bound in Great Britain
by Wm Collins Sons & Co Ltd, Glasgow

Contents

Preface

'I don't know what you see in rugby,' my wife said. 'It's always the same – a lot of hyperthyroids dashing about in their underwear.'

'Ah, but it's not always the same,' I told her. 'The great thing about rugby is the way it keeps surprising you. I mean, look at Dennis Kilbey.'

'I might,' she said. 'It depends. Is he in his underwear?'

'Dennis Kilbey,' I said, 'is one of the game's immortals. He captained Boscastle Nomads the day they got thrashed by Newquay Reserves, largely because he miscounted his team before the kick-off and then he ran the touch while they played with fourteen men. You don't get that sort of originality,' I pointed out, 'in tennis.'

'You don't get kicked in the slats in tennis, either,' she said.

'And take Paul Camp,' I went on. 'Guaranteed a place in rugby's Hall of Fame, that man. He was playing on the wing for Old Reedonians versus Reigate when the referee's dog came up and sank its teeth in his leg. Camp roundly cursed the animal, and the referee immediately threatened to send him off for misconduct. There's loyalty for you! It's Law 26(3)(j) if you want to look it up.'

'I'm white-hot,' she said, 'with apathy. If you ask me, once rugby players have succeeded in getting their boots on the right feet, the mental challenge of the game is largely over.'

'That's completely unfair!' I protested. 'What about slicing up the oranges?'

'And the way most of them run,' she added, 'I sometimes think they failed the first test.'

'Listen, some very great men have played rugby,' I declared. 'What about Reginald Armstrong, capped by England in 1925? At the age of sixty-nine he became the first doctor in Great Britain ever to diagnose Foot-and-Mouth Disease in man!'

'Which team's changing-room was he in at the time?' she asked, which proves that women have no sporting instinct at all. As soon as they think they're losing, they cheat. That's why they never understand rugby. Waste of time trying to explain, really.

Nevertheless, that conversation led me to reconsider my attitude towards the game. What is it that rugby has which the other sports lack? Apart, that is, from a neat row of stud-marks across the back and a colourful exhibition of scar-tissue down both shins.

Take soccer. Not a bad game, soccer. The kit they wear is quite pretty, if you go in for gaudy silks and satins; and it's a good way of learning your geography. Would anyone have heard of Accrington without Stanley or of Partick without Thistle? All the same, they do make a lot of noise when they play. Soccer has been aptly described as twenty-two refs and one complete pratt. And what actually goes on when one of them scores and all his team-mates climb on top of him? Is it true that they shut their eyes when they kiss?

On the face of it, hockey seems a decent enough game. I reject entirely the comment of the man who claimed that all the players are as bent as their sticks. This was a personal expression of his disgruntlement after he had mis-timed a shot and hit himself on the left knee-cap with a crack like a splitting coconut, after which both teams totally ignored him and he had to crawl to the pavilion on all fours. All threes, actually.

Well, that was his bad luck, but all the same there is something deeply suspect about hockey. Any game that can fill Wembley Stadium with tens of thousands of fanatical schoolgirls must be unhealthy.

There is, of course, another form of hockey: ice-hockey. 'Knives on their feet and clubs in their hands,' was how one man described it to me, and I don't think there is anything to add to that.

I will deal briefly with two other masochistic sports – golf (a good walk spoilt), and cross-country running (a bad walk spoilt) – and move quickly to cricket.

One thing in favour of cricket is its unique spiritual quality. The English, being an unimaginative people, have no conception of eternity; that's why they invented cricket. Unfortunately it appeals to all the worst instincts in the people who play it. There are only two types of cricketers: the selfish (batting and bowling) and the servile (fielding). It is impossible to decide which is worse.

Sailing. Is sailing a sport? I suppose so. However, there's no point in wasting much time over its curious appeal. Sailing under canvas is like standing in a cold shower while throwing away pound notes. Power-boat racing is like being hosed down by riot police while throwing away fivers. Either way, it's worth remembering W. C. Fields' remark about being in a boat: that it has all the disadvantages of prison with the added danger of drowning.

Tennis, of course, has ceased to be a proper game at all, having become an extension of the Old Vic Theatre School. Squash, on the other hand, has rocketed in popularity. This is understandable if your idea of a good time is being locked in a room with a maniac whose only object is to hit the ball clean through the wall, even if it has to pass through you in the process.

Athletics? An impossible choice between emaciation (marathon; high jump) and elephantiasis (shot-putt), unless you want to be a sprinter, in which case you train endlessly for an event that lasts approximately ten seconds, and even if you win the thing it turns out that your girl-friend missed it all because she dropped her programme when the gun went off.

Swimming combines the worst features of athletics and sailing (see above).

That just about completes the list, I'm afraid, unless you want to enter the peculiar worlds of polo, scuba-diving, salmon-fishing, ballooning, or belting down the Cresta Run sitting behind a hyphenated Guards officer who thinks it's cissy to brake until the sled exceeds Mach 2. In any case, none of these pastimes offers the basic satisfaction which, in my experience, rugby alone can provide, and which is best summed up in the words of a 3rd XV captain I once knew.

As he watched his team wander on to the field, he said: 'Wonderful lot of blokes. They don't know the meaning of the word "fear".' Then he added: 'Come to that, there's not many words they do know the meaning of.' It's a humane game, rugby.

That's the reason behind this book. I wanted to describe how rugby happened, why it has flourished, and what special ingredient ensures that a good time is usually had by all, even though it looks like an awful brawl while it's happening.

Some of the contents first appeared elsewhere. The excerpt in 'Any colour you like as long as it's white' is from *I, George Nepia*, published by Herbert Jenkins, and the excerpt in 'The milk train versus the express' is Richard Burton's *The Immortal Dive of P.C. Mog*, from *The Barry John Book of Rugby*, published by Christopher Davies, Swansea. 'The underground lawbook', 'Fickle finger of fate' and 'On with the bawl' first appeared in *Rugby World* magazine, while 'What's Ellis all about?' is based on a talk I gave on BBC Radio 4. In each case, permission to reprint is gratefully acknowledged. Finally, my especial thanks to Mr Alf Wright, archivist to the RFU at Twickenham, amongst whose unique collection I passed many happy hours.

Sir William de Beaumont hears evidence at a West Country disciplinary committee from a player sent off for overacting; he got a 28-day suspension.

What's it all about, Ellis?

Let me make one thing very clear at the start (as politicians say while they're making up their minds which lie to tell). It is this. The Ancient Chinese did not do it. The Greeks did not do it. The medieval Gascons, Teutons, Tuscans, Saxons, Polacks, Switzers, Bulgars, Magyars, Latts, Finns or Croats did not do it. Nor, come to that, did the Dalmatians, Alsatians or Pomeranians do it, even when standing on their hind legs.

Nobody played rugby before the Brits did. Nobody.

I want to make this plain because people who write books about This Great Game of Ours always kick off with a chapter called Origins, and bloody boring it is.

They ramble on about how the Roman soldiers in Britain played *harpastum*, which was supposedly a kind of handball. So what? They had to do something while they were waiting for the hairy Picts to have another bash at Hadrian's Wall. It wasn't rugby.

Some historians attach great importance to a reference by Sir William de Beaumont (1473–1550) in his *Anatomie of Idlenesses*:

> 'One gayme veritably is a pestilence, wherein do lusty blaggards vent their beastely furie in dispewt over an leathern lumpe, and hereof groweth much bruising and murther, the cause of great rancour and malice, especialy when Bristol play Gloucester in a cup-tie.'

People who quote this as proof that the front rows were having a bit of a barney as long ago as the fifteenth century overlook the fact that the final eight words have been challenged by numerous experts who claim they were added at a much later date by someone with a red felt-tip pen who couldn't spell 'especially'.

The other thing that chroniclers of rugby always chuck in is Shrove Tuesday football. In various boring places like Chester and Derby they used to go mad on

Shrove Tuesday and fight all day for possession of a pig's bladder. This contest is said to have caused great amusement, although nobody ever noticed the pig laugh.

There's no evidence that any of it had anything to do with rugby. However, each year since the first sighting of Halley's Comet, a curious ceremony has taken place in the Somerset village of Nempnett Thrubwell. On the Fifth Sunday after the Middlesex Sevens, fifteen villagers gather at one end of the High Street and shout, 'Knock-on, ref!' while another fifteen gather at the other end and shout back, 'What about the off-side, then?' After that they all go off and get drunk.

The reasons for this curious ritual are lost in the mists of time. In my opinion it had something to do with establishing the right to sell buttered parsnips outside licensing hours. In any case rugby didn't come into it, because rugby didn't come into anything until Victoria was well and truly on the throne. (Forget William Webb Ellis. I'll sort him out later.) Anything that happened before Victoria can safely be ignored.

What is also clear is that there was precious little handling in the game in the first half of the nineteenth century. A player might catch the ball, make a mark and drop-kick or place-kick for goal; but it wasn't the done thing to run with the ball. Thomas Hughes, who wrote *Tom Brown's School Days*, remembered:

> 'In my first year, 1834, running with the ball to get a try was not absolutely forbidden, but a jury of Rugby boys of that day would almost certainly have found a verdict of "justifiable homicide" if a boy had been killed in running in.'

Even more telling is a description of the game that Hughes gives in his novel. At a line-out there is a rush that takes the ball 'right through the School line'. A boy called Brooke is 'close upon it' and goes 'straight for the School goal-posts'. He survives an attempted tackle. 'And now he is close to the School goal, *the ball not three yards before him*.' The defenders fail to stop him: 'no one throws himself on the ball, the only chance, and young Brooke has touched it right under the School goal-posts.'

Hughes wasn't describing a handling attack. Apart from the line-out and the final touch-down it sounded much more like a game of soccer, with Brooke dribbling the ball past defenders. However, running with the ball began to become more popular in the later 1830s, so much so that in the 1840s there were several attempts to settle the laws of the game for all time (a practice that is still going on). For example, it was agreed in 1842 that 'running-in' – that is, carrying the ball over the goal to score – was allowed provided the ball had been caught on the bound, the player was on-side, and he didn't 'hand it on' (pass it) but ran in and scored himself. Picking up from the ground was definitely illegal.

In 1846 there was another major attempt to define the game at Rugby School. It produced thirty-seven written rules. Rule 7 is interesting:

> 'Knocking on, as distinguished from throwing on, is altogether disallowed . . . '

That didn't necessarily mean then what it seems to mean now. In those days 'fist-punting' was a recognised way of moving the ball in the football played at other schools, such as Westminster: you held the ball in one hand and punched it away with the other, a technique still used in Australian Rules football. Maybe that was what Rule 7 meant by 'knocking on'. In any case there were other, far more important, points to be settled:

> *Rule 13.*
> It is not fair to hack and hold at the same time.

Rule 19.
It shall be a goal if the ball goes over the bar (whether it touches or not) without having touched the dress or person of any player; but no player may stand on the goal bar to interrupt it going over.

(Presumably somebody had done this.)

Rule 23.
No agreement between two players to send the ball straight out shall be allowed.

(This is curious. Did it mean agreement between two team-mates or between a player and his opponent? Either way, it's hard to understand what was going on, or why.)

Rule 24.
A player having touched the ball straight for a tree and touched the tree with it, may drop from either side if he can, but one of the opposite side may oblige him to go to his own side of the tree.

(In fact there were three full-sized elm trees growing just inside the touchline in midfield on the Rugby School ground. Rule 24 makes it sound as if when a ball were kicked into a tree the same player got the ball again; but according to a later account it was anybody's ball: '. . . the elements of chance came prominently into play as each side stood below, watching the ball fall from branch to branch.' The last of these elms came down in 1893.)

Rule 25.
No hacking with the heel or above the knee is fair.

Rule 28.
No player may wear projecting nails or iron plates on the soles or heels of his shoes or boots.

Rule 32.
All matches are drawn after 5 days or after 3 days if no goal has been kicked.

By 1846 two other essential features had developed: the H-shaped goal posts and a scoring system that depended on kicking goals over the crossbar. But those were just cosmetic details. What the game was all about was scrummaging. Here's Thomas Hughes again:

No lack of trees on or about the field in this match at Rugby in 1870, but even more interesting is the ball: big as a melon and just as round.

'The ball has just fallen . . . and they close rapidly around it in a scrummage. It must be driven through now by force or skill . . . Look how differently the boys face it. Here come two of the bull-dogs, bursting through the outsiders: in they go, straight to the heart of the scrummage, bent on driving the ball out on the opposite side.'

The scrummage wasn't a way of restarting play; it was almost the whole point and purpose of going out to play in the first place. And scrummaging was not the modern business of getting low and shoving hard; it was a barbaric test of raw courage and stoic indifference to pain that came when large numbers of players stood upright in a mob and hacked their way forward, often wearing iron-tipped boots known at Rugby School as 'navvies' (and never mind what the rules said).

15

When B. Fletcher Robinson wrote a book called *Rugby Football* in 1896, here's how he remembered those days:

> 'This hacking was the worst feature of the game. It was useful in one respect, for without it the ball might never have emerged from the forest of legs which concealed it. It seems to have originated at Rugby School. The hacking there was indeed of a terrible nature. To hack hard and take your punishment manfully seems to have been the end and object of the play. Two boys would often be seen steadily hacking each other long after the ball and the forwards had passed to the other side of the ground. Personal disputes were sometimes settled in this rough and ready fashion. Of course some elderly football players, whose old triumphs, as seen through the softening haze of the past, awake nothing but pleasant memories, are still willing to contend that the hacking system was neither dangerous nor brutal. This is simply absurd. Many an Old Rugbeian can show scars existing today which are the relics of wounds received under the old barbarous rules. There is no doubt that accidents were of very common occurrence, and that the majority of them were due to hacking and hacking alone. The first upward step that Rugby football made from brutalism to science was the abolition of the entire system of hacking an opponent in the scrum or tripping him up when he was running with the ball. Mr Arthur C. Guillemard, in Mr Marshall's *History of Football,* relates an anecdote from his personal experience which throws more light on this style of play than anything I can say. "I well remember," he writes, "seeing the crack 'hack' of one season, after coming through the scrummage, finish off his triumphal march by place-kicking the half-back in front of me clean off his legs" – a pleasant picture of football as it was played in the sixties.'

If that sounds exaggerated, read an Old Rugbeian's views of the game as played in the late 1850s; he was writing in 1860, so his memory was fresh and his images vivid:

> 'You should just have seen the scrummages in the Sixth Match two years ago . . . Fellows did not care a fig for the ball then except inasmuch as it gave them a decent pretext for hacking. I remember a scrummage! . . . we'd been hacking for five minutes already, and

hadn't had half enough, in fact, the swells had only just begun to warm to their work, when a bystander . . . kindly . . . informed us that the ball was waiting our convenience on top of the island . . . And then there was Hookey Walker, the swell hack on the Sixth side; my eye! didn't he walk into the School! only shut up ten fellows for the season, and sent half a dozen home for the rest of the half . . . merely to see him come through a scrummage was the signal for all the ladies to shriek and faint. Bless you, my dear fellow, they enjoy looking on at a scrummage of all things now – more shame to us. And there was none of that underhand shuffling play with the ball then that there is now; no passing it along from one to the other; all was manly and straightforward. Why, to let the ball go after you had once got into a scrummage was considered to be as flagrant a transgression of the rules of football as to take it up when you were off your side. Nor did you see any of that shirking outside scrummages that's always going on nowadays. No one thought you worth your salt if you weren't the colour of your mother earth from head to toe ten minutes after the match had begun. But, dash my buttons! you haven't a chance of getting a decent fall in the present day; and no wonder either when you see young dandies "got up regardless of expense", mincing across Big Side, and looking just as if their delicate frames wouldn't survive any violent contact with the ball. Hang the young puppies! We shall have fellows playing in dress boots and lavender-coloured kid gloves before long . . . My maxim is hack the ball on when you see it near you, and when you don't, why then hack the fellow next you.'

That described the way the game was played at its birthplace only a dozen years before the RFU was founded. More boot than anything else was involved. Meanwhile, at other schools and at Oxbridge, variants of football were being played, and in the 1860s there was a determined attempt to agree on a common code that would bring them all together in a Football Association. It failed: supporters of the 'Rugby game' insisted on being allowed to handle, to score goals *above* the crossbar, above all to hack; while the Association footballers rejected all these and disliked the peculiar shape of the oval ball too. The two styles were irreconcilable. Association became soccer, and rugby went its own sweet way. More from Fletcher Robinson:

'In 1865 there were but fifteen to twenty clubs round London playing Rugby football. Nearly all the teams were composed of young men who learnt the game at the two great football schools, Rugby and Marlborough. The Richmond team in that year, for instance, was entirely composed of Old Rugbeians and Old Marlburians. The rules were in a very uncertain state, and the opposing captains often met to decide the minor points before the game commenced. The grounds about London were unenclosed, and the spectators seem to have wandered about at their own sweet will. Indeed, a smart half often availed himself of the protection of the crowd to dash in near the touch-line before the unfortunate back opposed to him could find out exactly where he was. The number of players was uncertain but usually twenty a side. The off-side laws were very lax, and some clubs would send down an advance guard of forwards to protect the man running with the ball. This fact is rather interesting, because the Americans adopted the same plan, and have never changed it. In Yankee football the protection of the man with the ball is all important, and for this purpose their systems of wedges and lines of covering forwards were invented. The scrummages were long, tedious bouts of hard shoving. The men did not put their heads down, but stood upright and hacked and pushed their way blindly forward.'

It couldn't last. One of the first things the RFU did in 1871 was prohibit hacking and tripping. (Abolishing them took rather longer: many people rather enjoyed inflicting and receiving pain. The Victorians were a funny lot.) At first the change made the game worse in one respect. Without the galvanising effects of hacking, the scrummages lasted even longer (and they had never been speedy affairs: even before 1871, spectators used to take out their pocket-watches and time the scrummages, in minutes). Speaking at the Edinburgh Academicals jubilee dinner in 1908, Sir J. H. A. Macdonald looked back at the way rugby was played in the 1880s:

'Very few present had seen a real scrum. Had they ever seen a haycock that had been put up when the hay was wet, and the smoke or steam was rising from it? That was just like a scrum in those days, and it was just about as motionless.'

18

It doesn't sound very exciting. It wasn't very exciting. To state the case plainly, it was tedious. The game that the RFU adopted in 1871 had so many things wrong with it that the wonder is anyone played, let alone watched.

When the RFU celebrated its centenary, a bunch of people formed what they called the XX Club to mark the occasion. It was XX because they played demonstration matches according to the 1871 laws of the game – twenty a side. I saw a couple of those games, and very boring they were. Forty players made a crowded field. Attacks soon ran out of space and were stifled. With up to fourteen forwards from each side packing down in the scrums, the ball took a long time to emerge. There was much congestion and confusion, and because the two captains did their own refereeing, play was less than fluid. Often it was gelid.

In the beginning, rugby was a pretty awful game. We can see that now. Virtually all the many changes made to the laws have been for the good. We should be grateful for the pioneer work of those early forwards who spent most of the match blindly heaving and straining, while the backs patiently waited for a ball which they dared not pass for fear of being labelled a 'funk'. And we should be twice as grateful for being lucky enough to play a much better game of rugby now.

An 1871 scrum working up a good head of steam. Now that hacking was banned, the ball probably wouldn't emerge for several minutes, long enough for the chap on the left to complete his impression of a penguin.

Most games were not invented; they just developed. Nobody gets the credit for having dreamed up golf or cricket or hockey. Rugby is different. Not only was it named after Rugby School, said to have been its birthplace; there was also a boy at the school who is commemorated as the originator of the game. Very few rugby players haven't heard of William Webb Ellis who, according to a plaque in a wall

near the headmaster's house, in 1823 'with a fine disregard for the rules of football as played in his time first took the ball in his arms and ran with it, thus originating the distinctive feature of the Rugby game'. The extraordinary thing is that nobody thought this incident worth recording *at the time.*

Considering the revolutionary implications of what Ellis is supposed to have done, you'd think someone would have scribbled a note in his diary, or mentioned it in a letter home: 'Played football this afternoon, and Ellis cheated awfully by holding the ball and running with it, though some of the other chaps thought this was a spiffing idea. Wonder if it will catch on?' That sort of comment. But no. Ellis's act of fine disregard left absolutely no contemporary record at all. Indeed it wasn't until seventy-two years had passed that the Old Rugbeians' Society set up a committee of inquiry into the origins of rugby football, and by then William Webb Ellis had long since gone to his Maker.

Not surprisingly, the committee failed to find any eye-witnesses who could corroborate the story; equally unsurprisingly, if you bear in mind that rugby football had by then become an important sport and the committee was made up of old Rugbeians, they gave all the credit for this great game to Rugby School in general and Ellis in particular. Well, I don't believe the second part. It seems a remarkable feat of detection to go back seventy-two years and discover an event that was supposed to have had startling consequences and yet not be able to produce a shred of first-hand evidence that it ever happened. I realise the scientific impossibility of proving a negative, so I'm not about to insist that William Webb Ellis did not take the ball in his arms and run with it in 1823. What I will say is that nobody has ever got within a hundred miles of proving that he did, or even of establishing a strong likelihood that he did; so I believe it's fair to say that the William Webb Ellis story is a myth.

There's quite a bit of circumstantial evidence to indicate that Ellis was a most improbable inventor of rugby. For one thing, he never had a name as a footballer at Rugby School. For another, he was only a day-boy, and day-boys carried much less social weight than boarders. It doesn't add up to the identikit picture of a trendsetter, especially when you consider what a major change Ellis is supposed to have made. The game of football as played at Rugby in the 1820s didn't have many rules, but one rule was that running with the ball was banned and if you did it you were asking to get kicked, hacked and generally cut down to size, kicking and hacking being highly-rated skills in those days.

Thomas Hughes, the author of *Tom Brown's Schooldays,* attended Rugby about ten years after the alleged Ellis incident. In 1895 the old Rugbeians' committee of inquiry asked him for his views. He made it clear that, although running with the ball was not absolutely forbidden in his day, it was considered an extraordinary, even suicidal, thing to do.

So, if Ellis had no great sporting ability or personal prestige to protect him, he was living very dangerously if he did what he's said to have done. What's more, he seems to have taken not the slightest interest in Rugby football after 1823. He went to Oxford, wrote an ode to ale while he was at Brasenose College, played cricket – he was good enough to bat first wicket down against Cambridge and score twelve runs – took Holy Orders, was rector of various churches, lived a long and comfortable life, and died in the South of France in 1872, one year after the Rugby Football Union was formed. By that time international matches were being played, but whether or not word of these resounding developments reached Ellis we shall never know. He left £9000, which was a lot of money in those days, but as to his views on rugby football he left nothing at all.

So what have we got? A boy who makes no mark on school sport until suddenly he has a brainstorm and does something very risky, which, it is claimed, ultimately transforms a game in which he himself thereafter takes not the slightest interest. Not the most convincing scenario, but stranger things had happened at Rugby School: they had two rebellions there between 1778 and 1794: it was quite a volatile place. But that's not the end of the evidence. That fine, iconoclastic journalist, the late J. L. Manning, once took a long, hard look at the Old Rugbeians' committee of inquiry of 1895. He investigated the investigators, and he concluded that they had wilfully falsified the history of rugby, as he put it, 'by needlessly dishonest methods which stopped just short of forgery but not of distortion and suppression and the harassing of a dying witness . . . ' 'Almost,' Manning added, 'the perfect hoax.'

What he'd found was this. A certain Martin Bloxam created the legend of William Webb Ellis fifty years after the alleged event. Bloxam was a solicitor and antiquarian who'd left Rugby in 1820, so although he may have known Ellis he certainly never saw him do the deed in 1823. In 1876 Bloxam wrote an account of it for the school magazine – but he wasn't sure of the date and he gave no source for his information: an odd way for an antiquarian to behave, as J. L. Manning pointed out. Nothing happened for the next twenty years. Then a man called Shearman wrote a history of football in which he suggested that the Rugby game was merely a modern version of a primitive form.

The book appeared at a particularly sensitive time. The game was rapidly slipping out of the hands of the men who considered themselves its rightful owners. After all, it was three old Rugbeians who had drafted the laws of the game when the Rugby Football Union was formed in 1871. Ten of the England XX against Scotland in 1871 had been Old Rugbeians. Sixteen Old Rugbeians played in the Oxford XX that beat Cambridge in the first University match, in 1872, and the first five presidents of the RFU were all Old Rugbeians. It was, clearly, 'the Rugby game'; but in the eighties and nineties lesser breeds without the law – that is, working-class northerners – had begun laying claim to it. Rugby had become popular up there. The public-school ethos of the game for the game's sake was being challenged by a commercial spirit that treated rugby as a spectator sport, and the Old Rugbeians resented this attempted takeover. It was no coincidence that they set up their committee of inquiry in 1895 – the year of the split between the RFU and the northern clubs who later formed the Rugby League. The Old Rugbeians were reclaiming their sacred heritage. It would help enormously if they could prove that it was really theirs.

The committee promptly dug up the Martin Bloxam story.

Bloxam himself was dead by now, but Thomas Hughes (of *Tom Brown's Schooldays*) was still alive, so the committee asked him for confirmation. Hughes not only told them he'd never heard of Ellis as a footballer, he also wrote: 'I don't think Matt Bloxam a trustworthy authority,' and he added crushingly: 'The William Webb Ellis tradition had not survived to my day' – and Hughes, remember, went to the school only seven years after the supposed Ellis incident.

When the committee published their report, none of that information was included. It wasn't the proof they sought, so they ignored it. Worse, they also ignored evidence that named another man altogether, Theodore Walrond, as the *real* pioneer of rugby football. This revelation came from a George Benn, who had entered Rugby School in 1830. He vividly recalled what the football was like, but The Event (as the committee called Ellis's alleged act) meant nothing to him. 'Before Benn left,' so the committee's notes read, 'Theodore Walrond introduced a system of backs and half-backs and after leaving Oxford sent down a set of draft rules on approval. Benn is convinced that Theodore Walrond perfected the game and deserves the credit.' That, too, was left out of the committee's report. Nevertheless they had high hopes of an old clergyman, the Rev. Thomas Harris, the only man still alive who had been at school with William Webb Ellis.

Harris was eighty-three and dying but the committee badgered him with calls and letters. They were determined to find some testimony that would buttress their claim. When they wrote to a man who was interrogating Harris for them, the letter reveals more than a hint of their desperation:

'I wonder if Mr Harris thoroughly understands what we are at? Did you explain there was a tradition, etc., to be found in

Bloxam's book . . . It is not for me to suggest what you should do, but I should press him . . . he must remember Our Hero doing something unusual.'

But Harris remembered no such thing, and he refused to be bullied. He simply repeated that he remembered Ellis only as a cricketer, and when the committee kept pressing him he very wisely withdrew almost everything he had said on the subject.

Harris, and George Benn, and Thomas Hughes, had died by the time the committee's report came out, which meant there was nobody left to expose it for the swindle it was.

Not that it mattered. Long before all the evidence had been collected, let alone assessed, the committee had made up their mind what their decision would be, and had ordered a local mason to cut the commemorative stone that is now at the bottom of the headmaster's garden. Quite right too. When you're manufacturing a myth, what you need most of all is bags of confidence. The facts can come a little bit later.

There is an interesting parallel to the Ellis myth in America, and curiously enough it happened at about the same time. Towards the end of the nineteenth century, when baseball was developing into a major sport, Americans came to believe that a man called Abner Doubleday invented the game in 1839. At the time he had been an instructor at a military prep school. Later, as a Civil War general, he fought in the battle of Gettysburg, heroically by all accounts; but it was what he was said to have done in the summer of 1839 that made him enduringly famous throughout the United States.

The legend said that Abner Doubleday laid out the first-ever baseball field and on it he conducted the first game of baseball ever played. This was in Coopers-town, then a village in upper New York State. The place became a baseball shrine. In 1920 Doubleday Field was declared a permanent memorial, and in 1930 the National Baseball Hall of Fame was dedicated at Cooperstown. Everyone – certainly all the major league clubs – saluted Abner Doubleday's inspiration and genius.

Then the historians got into the act, and the legend was exposed for what it was: a legend.

There is no shortage of clear references to baseball long before 1839. A bestseller called *The Boy's Own Book*, published in London in 1828, described rounders as a game played on a diamond with a base at each corner; the ball had to be hit over the diamond or it was a foul; if the batter struck at the ball and missed three times he was out; if he hit the ball and it was caught on the full he was out. Clearly rounders was just a different name for baseball.

In any case the word 'baseball' went back much further. Jane Austen used it in *Northanger Abbey* in 1798. Fifty years earlier, Lady Hervey described in a letter what the family of Frederick, Prince of Wales, were doing: they were 'diverting themselves with baseball, a play all who are or have been schoolboys are well acquainted with'. And in 1744 an alphabetical book of sports for English children – the kind that starts 'A is for Archery' – chose to represent the letter B with Baseball.

The need to create a creator, along the lines of Ellis or Doubleday, is so strong that sociologists have given it a name: *reductionist origin myth*. No doubt it's a harmless delusion, rather like believing – as a remarkably large number of people do – that the Queen of England has supernatural or quasi-divine qualities. But two things are remarkable about the Ellis affair.

One is that so many Old Rugbeians could cheat, lie and swindle with such enthusiasm, all in the name of preserving the ideals of fair play and sportsmanship. The other is that the myth they manufactured has lasted so long. It was clever of the Old Rugbeians to make Ellis a rebel, a man 'with a fine disregard for the rules'. Everyone loves a rebel. And who would suspect the Old Rugbeians of themselves disregarding the rules of historical investigation, when they honoured a rebel? Very cunning, that.

Everyone knows that Welsh rugby is the only truly popular version of the game, having 'sprung from the loins of the valleys, sired by *hwyl* out of *eirith*, forged in the Celtic furnace, and flowering like a great golden tidal wave that enshrines the soaring eagle-spirit of *Cymri*' – Rev. Dafydd ap ffestiniog, noted fifteenth-century bard.

What the poet was trying to say was that in Wales the rugby came up through the people, whereas in England and Scotland it has been grudgingly released from the manicured grip of an upper-class public-school-educated minority, the kind of

people who each have six bank accounts, talk without moving their lips, and keep their hanky tucked up their sleeve (or, in Scotland, stuffed in their sporran).

This (Welshmen believe) explains why they (the Welsh) are so much better at the game.

The English – according to the Authorized Welsh Version – ponce about the field, crosseyed from inbreeding, and get a nasty headache if asked to do two things at once, such as catch the ball and run.

The Scots – again, this is the official Viet Taff view – haven't completely recovered from the culture shock they underwent in 1933 when their national team first wore numbered jerseys. Until then, Scottish officials had regarded numbered jerseys as a sickening betrayal of the true amateur spirit of the game, and even today there are those at Murrayfield who regret the change and who think the whole game would be vastly improved if the selectors refused to consider anyone other than property-owners with, say, five thousand a year clear.

(It is not widely known that in 1933 the Welsh team was still playing in *lettered* jerseys. This was a tactical dodge, adopted to avoid possible embarrassment. Half the team were still counting on their fingers, which meant they couldn't get above ten without risking arrest for indecent exposure.)

Which leaves the Irish, plus various colonial teams. The Welsh refuse to take the Irish seriously, even if the Irish win. This all dates back to 1903. In that year, when the Irish RFU held its annual meeting, the treasurer had to explain why the dinner after the match with Scotland had cost £50 while the bill for the Welsh team's dinner had been only £30:

> 'The reason for this was that champagne was given to the Scotsmen and beer only (but plenty of it) to the Welshmen. Whisky and porter were always good enough for Welshmen, for such were the drinks they were used to. The Scotsmen, however, were gentlemen, and appreciated a dinner when it was given to them. Not so the Welshmen.'

(That must be true, because I found it in the official history of the Welsh Rugby Union.)

But what everyone knows about Welsh rugby is not so. It is a myth. Indeed it is *two* myths. Welsh rugby did not spring from the common people; it sprang from the upper classes, and especially from their public-school-and-Oxbridge-educated sons. And in the beginning Welsh rugby was not even Welsh; it was largely English. Which is not really surprising, because much of South Wales was peopled by English immigrants.

In 1870 – when Lancashire and Yorkshire were playing county matches, and there was already so much club rugby that within the next five years England, Scotland and Ireland were to form their rugby unions – there was virtually no rugby in Wales. The boom that brought the game in its wake was just beginning.

As the Klondike had a gold rush, so South Wales had a coal rush. It sucked in men from all around, a great tidal wave of humanity surging up the valleys and changing the character of the country as they altered its economy. No part of Britain felt the impact of the industrial revolution more than this. When Victoria became queen, Wales was largely an agricultural country. Few roads crossed it; the best routes were the old drover roads, ancient cattle trails that led over the mountains into England. At the start of the century Cardiff and Newport were little more than villages, each with a population of a couple of thousand. At first the coal rush attracted people from the Welsh countryside. But the demand kept doubling and redoubling: the railways kept probing further and further up the valleys: all the world wanted Welsh coal, and there weren't enough Welshmen to dig it. After 1870 the influx of Englishmen year by year matched the drift from the Welsh countryside; and when you added the Scots and Irish there were more foreigners than natives moving into the boom belt. Not surprisingly, a great number of those Englishmen came from the nearby counties of Gloucestershire, Somerset, Devon and Cornwall. They didn't speak Welsh, and they weren't about to learn it. By the turn of the century, something like a million people had arrived in South Wales in forty years. Newport and Cardiff had mushroomed to populations of over 100,000 each (and were still growing). But they were not native Welshmen. In Cardiff only eight people in a hundred could speak Welsh; in Newport, the figure was half that. Further west it was a different story. In the Rhondda, two out of three spoke Welsh, and in Llanelli virtually everyone did. But rugby did not spring from west Wales. It came out of the east, because it came out of England; and in the beginning Wales were glad to select a remarkably large number of unmistakeably English players to wear the scarlet jersey.

For what they're worth – which is not a lot – the records show that St David's College, Lampeter, introduced rugby to Wales in 1850. It was probably a fairly shambolic game, since they'd got it from Cambridge where the rules were pretty casual. A few schools took it up – Llandovery College; Christ College, Brecon; Monmouth School – and it seems pretty certain that when Welsh clubs were formed it was the old boys of these establishments who formed them. It's significant, for instance, that when Cardiff played away for the first time it was against Cowbridge Grammar School.

That was in 1876, by which time the South Wales Football Club had been set up. Its aim was to pick the best team available and play the top clubs in the west of England and nearby. Anyone who wanted to be considered for selection had to send the secretary five shillings. Five shillings then was worth ten pounds today, which says something about the social standing of the members. But then, most clubs were staunchly middle-class. Swansea was originally a cricket club; it was the cricketers who decided to play rugby at St Helens. Cricket had been played on Cardiff Arms Park since 1845; the winter game was a late addition. Newport was first known as the 'Newport Cricket, Athletic, Football and Tennis Club'. (Many Welsh clubs still have the word 'Athletic' in their name.) When clubs like Neath and Llanelli were founded the impulse came from above, not below; and often it was a foreigner who had the idea. T. P. Whittington, capped by Scotland in 1873, was Neath's first captain. Buchanan, another Scot, led Llanelli in their first season, and several more Scots helped him.

Most of the founder-members were professional men – lawyers and doctors and so on – and most of the backing they got came from the rich and influential. In the very beginning, Welsh rugby clubs got off the ground because old boys of the public schools attracted the patronage of well-to-do gentry or ambitious industrialists who could afford to help with the expenses. At that time, the man in the street didn't have a look-in. Nor did he seem to want one. Rugby was a game for Oxbridge graduates who could afford the time off to play it. (There is a story that when Neath toured Devon in 1887, the party set off without E. V. Pegge, who was late; so he chartered a special train to catch up with them. Neath was by no means a working-class club.)

The first change came with the formation of the Welsh Rugby Union. Paradoxically, it began as a thoroughly class-conscious body, anxious to be socially acceptable to the rest of the rugby world, especially England.

It began with a man called Richard Mullock. He was Newport's secretary, and he took a dim view of the South Wales Football Club which, even when it changed its name to 'Union', couldn't seem to get anything right. In February 1880 it sent a team to play Gloucester. The selectors had cocked it up again: there was a fixture clash, the best Welsh players were elsewhere, Gloucester romped home. Welsh rugby was rubbished again.

Mullock had had enough. Within a month he fixed up a meeting at the Tenby Hotel, Swansea, where various interested parties put their heads together to decide what ought to be done. Mullock came away with the clear impression that they had authorised him to contact the Rugby Football Union, arrange an England–Wales match and raise a Wales XV to play in it. Later, other people remembered differently but by then it was too late: Mullock had written to

Richard Mullock, the
father of Welsh rugby:
never mind the score, get
on with the diplomacy!

London asking for the game. In this respect he was typical of so many reckless and foolhardy individuals without whom rugby would never have got off the ground. Like them, Mullock behaved irresponsibly, he failed to consult others, and before long he showed himself to be a truly lousy administrator; but at least *he got things going*. Other people could follow and straighten out the mess. It took men like Mullock to make a start.

He arranged a trial which of course never happened. The actual match was postponed twice. The final date was 19 February 1881. This was also the date of a semi-final cup-tie between Swansea and Llanelli, but he pressed on regardless.

It was said afterwards that the game was not a true England–Wales international, just a turn-out by an England side against 'a private team got up by Mullock'. There is some truth in this. Mullock seems to have picked the team, somewhat absentmindedly, when he had nothing else to do. Those who found themselves representing Wales couldn't quite describe how it had happened. 'Some individual would have a conversation with you,' one player remarked, 'take your name and address, and pass on . . . ' Another recollected: 'It was mentioned to me that . . . I had been chosen to play for Wales . . . ' Thus selection was vague in the extreme. 'I had no definite instructions,' one player said.

The whole set-up was indefinite. Who did the team represent? Not the South Wales Football Union, obviously. Not the Welsh Rugby Union, which had yet to be formed. (It came into being a month later, at a meeting in the Castle Hotel, Neath.) England certainly thought they were playing Wales; but it was a very odd

Welsh team that ran on to Richardson's Field in Blackheath. Two players, for instance, had come to watch. While the Welshmen were changing in the Princess of Wales pub, they realised they were two short, so a couple of Welsh students got recruited from the crowd. The line-up had to be rejigged to accommodate them. Newman of Newport went to full-back for the first (and only) time, and Treharne of Pontypridd, normally a half-back, became a forward.

Ten minutes after the kick-off, a half-back (Lewis, of Llandovery) and a forward (Mann, of Cardiff) got crocked. Soon Wales were down to thirteen men again. One of those was Godfrey Darbishire of Bangor, who hadn't played rugby for two years. In the circumstances, the Welshmen did well to hold England to a dropped goal and thirteen tries, seven of them converted. (One press report said that the best Welsh forward was Treharne, the ex-halfback.)

I doubt if Mullock was terribly worried by the score. He never really expected to win, and in any case he knew that what mattered was not the result but that Wales should be seen capable of playing the game *in the proper way*.

The men who had shaped the rugby unions of England and Scotland were public-school products. It was important for Wales to show that they knew how to talk their language. Mullock's team contained nine Oxbridge men, plus one educated at Cheltenham College and an old boy of Monmouth School. Moreover it didn't just represent the industrial belt. Llandovery had two players; Haverford-west and Bangor one each. Perhaps Darbishire, the Bangor man, wasn't fully fit – two years is a long lay-off – but in other respects he was admirably qualified. He was a Rugby-and-Balliol man; his family owned large parts of Caernarvonshire. He might be a bit slow around the field but old Darbishire was a jolly good chap.

They were all good chaps. This was a team of gentlemen who knew how to play the game, on and off the field, not a bunch of Celtic buffoons. You could tell the difference just by looking at them. The hapless squads of the South Wales Football Union had worn vests of black, decorated with a white leak: charmingly ethnic, if you liked that sort of thing, but not *chic*. Mullock's Wales XV appeared in pure scarlet jerseys that bore the heraldic emblem of the Prince of Wales: a flourish of feathers with the words 'Ich Dien', meaning 'I serve'.

Now that was a masterstroke of diplomacy. The rugby establishment gathered at Blackheath must have found it very reassuring. It showed that these Welsh fellows could be trusted. They not only had manners, they had taste.

And they had friends in high places. The first president of the WRFU was as great a peer of the realm as you could find. The Earl of Jersey could trace his ancestry back to Henry VII. He'd been to Eton and Balliol. He had the equivalent of half a million in rents coming to him every year. He was the perfect choice.

So much for the myth that Welsh rugby sprang from the soil like an allotment of leeks. The truth is that Welsh rugby was a slavish imitation of the English model. The very last impression that Richard Mullock and his friends wanted to convey was one of originality.

They did, however, want to win before long.

Throughout the 1880s and 1890s, in their search for a winning team, the Welsh selectors were refreshingly open-minded about a candidate's origins. Their feeling was that a man who played rugby *in* Wales was qualified to play rugby *for* Wales. With that in mind they picked many an Englishman, such as F. E. Hancock of Cardiff, who was born in Wiveliscombe, Somerset; his brother actually played for England. Other Somerset men turned out for Wales: Boucher, Brice, Vile, the Biggs brothers, even the hyphenated Sweet-Escott, a name as English as Steele-Bodger. Wales picked Harry Uzzell from Gloucester, Dick Hellings from Tiverton, Tom Graham from Newcastle, Bert Winfield from Nottingham. Wallace Watts, who won a dozen Welsh caps in the early 1890s, came from Chipping Norton. Sam Ramsay of Treorchy – selected in 1896 – was a Scotsman. And so on and so on. It couldn't last, of course. As soon as Wales stopped losing – which didn't take long: they drew the game with England in 1887 and won by a try to nil in 1890 – the other Unions were bound to get a bit restless. But the WRFU knew where the balance of its playing strength lay, and right into the 1890s it kept lobbying the International Board to go on letting any Union pick its national team from its club players, no matter where they were born or who their parents were.

All that changed in the new century. The game became largely working-class and intensely, even narrowly Welsh. But the idea that it was originally created out of a passionate need for ordinary folk to express their Welsh identity is a myth. Welsh rugby was an import, a transplant, and during its first generation it survived because the national selectors had the wit to treat immigrants as honorary Welshmen.

The myth dies hard. It's often said, for instance, that during the war in South Africa the Welsh sided with the Boers, since they too were getting kicked about by the bloody English. The opposite was true. Wales was as gung-ho against the Boers as any nation; plenty of South Walians volunteered for the fight, and the Welsh Rugby Union gave £250 to help their dependents. When Watcyn Thomas (who captained Wales in the 1930s) came to write his autobiography he recalled a Swansea player 'whose uncle was the legendary Dai St John, who won an immortal place in Welsh legend for his fighting qualities in the Boer War, his favourite method of despatching his enemies being to bayonet them and throw them over his shoulder'. Not much sympathy for the underdog there.

Gung-ho!

Sport is said to be a substitute for war, which probably explains why so many sportsmen are so keen to enjoy the delights of the real thing when it comes along.

Rugby players in particular seem to make willing combatants. The list of medals won by men who have played for England includes one VC, thirty-two DSOs, thirty-one MCs and four DFCs. Plenty of Scots, Welsh, Irish and — as they used to be called — Dominion Caps earned decorations too (including the Irish internationals T. J. Crean and F. M. W. Harvey, who were each awarded the Victoria Cross).

Arthur Hartley was president of the RFU in 1914, and as soon as war was declared he wrote a circular urging rugby players to volunteer for service. Many did. John King of Headingley (twelve caps between 1911 and 1913 as a forward) immediately joined the Yorkshire Hussars as a trooper. He was killed in action in France on 9 August 1916. In 1911 King had been in the same team as the Harlequin wing-threequarter Douglas Lambert, when England demolished France 37-nil. Lambert was big. He scored two tries, kicked two penalties and five conversions, and set an England scoring record of 22 points that still stands. (Dusty Hare's 19 points against Wales in 1981 comes next.) Lambert was a lieutenant in the Buffs when he was killed in action near Loos on 13 October 1915.

The biographies of international players are dotted with that sort of information. Toggie Kendall and Bim Baxter, both of Birkenhead Park — selected by England at scrum-half and forward at the turn of the century — volunteered immediately. Toggie was thirty-six, Bim forty-four. Both were commissioned. Toggie went to the trenches with the King's Liverpool Regiment and was shot dead near Ypres on 25 January 1915. Bim served with the RNVR and survived to become an international referee, president of the RFU and manager of the 1930 British Lions. Such are the fortunes of war.

Then there was the splendidly named Roland Mangles (capped twice in 1897), who had been wounded once and decorated three times, including the DSO,

The England team that beat France 37–nil in 1911, Douglas Lambert's contribution being a record 22 points. Back F. M. Stoop, W. E. Mann, C. H. Pillman, A. D. Roberts, L. Haigh, Mr E. A. Johns; middle N. A. Wodehouse, D. Lambert, A. D. Stoop, J. G. G. Birkett (captain), R. Dibble, L. G. Brown, A. L. Kewney; front J. A. King, A. L. H. Gotley, S. H. Williams. Four of them, Pillman, Haigh, Lambert and King, were to lose their lives in the First World War.

before the First World War; during it he was mentioned in despatches no fewer than *eight times*: amazingly, he too survived. He retired as a brigadier-general. Robert Marshall was not so lucky. He won the first of his five caps in 1938 when he was still at Oxford. He was not yet twenty-one, but England picked him to play in the second row against Ireland at Dublin. England won 36-14, scoring seven tries. Marshall got the third. He ran fifty yards to score: not a thing many lock forwards do in their first international; he was being talked of as the new Wavell Wakefield when war broke out. He joined the Navy, became a lieutenant-commander, got the DSC and bar, and was killed in action on 12 May 1945 – four days after the war in Europe had been officially declared ended.

Another forward with the pace of a winger was the Irishman Tommy Crean, twice on the winning side when Ireland came to England in the 1890s. He had a tremendous build (6ft 2in) and great dash in both senses of the word. He went to South Africa with the 1896 Lions and stayed there. When the Boer War began, he

35

Robert Marshall, a lock forward who ran fifty yards to score in his first international.

Cyril Lowe, never dropped by England in ten years.

Douglas Kendrew: ten caps and four DSOs. Say no more.

joined the Imperial Light Horse as a trooper, although he was a fully qualified surgeon. In December 1901, at a spot called Tygerskloof, the Boers were hammering his unit, pouring in fire, knocking his men over. Crean — by now a captain — led from the front. He was hit but stayed on his feet, an example of defiance. The next bullet put him down. 'By Christ,' he shouted, 'I'm kilt entoirely!' The diagnosis proved faulty. He lived to collect not only the VC but also, in another war, the DSO and, after that, the Medal of the Humane Society for saving life at sea.

It may be unfair to single out individuals like this when so many fought and died; but who said life was fair? Certainly not Cyril Lowe, of Blackheath. First picked for the match against South Africa in January 1913, he hit peak form in 1914: two tries against Ireland, three against Scotland, three against France. Then came the war; there was to be no more international rugby until 1920. Lowe joined the Royal Flying Corps, shot down several German planes, won the MC and DFC, and came back to play in every England match until 1923. That meant he had never been dropped in a ten-year span: an astonishing achievement for a wing-threequarter who never weighed much more than 8½ stone. In his five years of international rugby he won twenty-five caps. Who knows? If there had been no war he might have doubled that number.

On the field Douglas Kendrew (Woodford, Leicester and the Army) was at the other end of the rugby spectrum from Lowe. Kendrew was a powerful and pugnacious prop at a time when England was producing jumbo packs. He played for England ten times in the thirties, including the Obolensky match when New Zealand was beaten 13-nil.

Blair Mayne:
unstoppable.

Gus Walker:
irrepressible.

The Distinguished Service Order is several cuts above the Distinguished Service Cross or the Distinguished Service Medal. It's not easy to win the Cross or the Medal, but the Order is awarded very sparingly indeed, and only after close scrutiny. On 1 June 1943 Kendrew won the DSO for gallantry in North Africa. On 13 January 1944 he won a second DSO for gallantry in Italy. On 4 May 1944 he won a third DSO for more of the same. And in 1953, when he was a brigade commander in Korea, he won his fourth DSO.

Four DSOs. It makes propping against the All Blacks seem like a holiday.

Kendrew's last game for England was in 1936, so he missed playing against Blair Mayne of Ireland, who won half a dozen caps at lock before the Second World War ended all that fun and games. Mayne was not especially huge for his position but he was very strong – some say the strongest man every to play for Ireland – and so brimming with energy that it was always likely to overflow unexpectedly. (After the 1938 match against Wales in Swansea he reportedly picked up a team-mate and flung him out of a window, either from excess of spirits or in response to some supposed slur; it happened to be a ground-floor window, but Mayne was unlikely to have considered that in advance.)

Such a forceful and restless temperament was not suited to conventional soldiering. Mayne went to North Africa and gravitated naturally to the SAS, which specialised in long-range desert patrols that carried raiding parties deep into enemy territory. Once, when Mayne had led a patrol that got inside a German airfield and destroyed a flock of aircraft, he came away with a control panel as a souvenir. What is remarkable is that he had ripped it out of the cockpit with his bare hands. By the end of the war he was a lieutenant-colonel with four DSOs.

Gus Walker played against Blair Mayne in the 1939 match at Twickenham. When he became president of the RFU in 1965 his full, formal title was Air Chief Marshal Sir George Augustus Walker, GCB, CBE, DSO, DFC, AFC, but to everyone in the rugby world he was Gus. Even for a fly-half he was small, and what little there was of him was further diminished in 1941 when he had an arm blown off by a bomb.

What happened – I heard this from a Marshal of the Royal Air Force, and I believe him – was that Gus, in command of a bomber base, was in the control tower one night watching a squadron take off. Something went badly wrong and a plane caught fire. He dashed across the field and was helping to pull out survivors when the blaze reached the bombs. Gus was actually blown clean over the control tower; he landed still conscious and intact, apart from the loss of an arm. (It sounds impossible, but such things happened.)

'He staggered back up into the control tower,' the Marshal of the RAF told me, 'and grabbed the phone to his group commander, and said: "Sir, d'you need a one-armed CO? Because now you've got one." Then he collapsed.'

Gus Walker couldn't play any more rugby, but he became a skilled and popular referee, especially during his presidential year; and I have a vivid memory of him at Twickenham, neatly anticipating a drop at goal and scudding to the posts as the ball sailed over.

And then there was Mobbs.

'Tall and strongly built, with weight and pace of that far-striding, high-stepping kind – all knees, as the saying goes – Mobbs was admirably adapted from a physical point of view for the position of wing-threequarter.'

Thus spoke the tireless E. H. D. Sewell in his *Rugby Football Roll of Honour 1914–1918*.

Edgar Mobbs was a hard man to stop. He scored six tries in a match on three occasions: twice as captain of East Midlands against Eastern Counties in 1907 and 1909, and once as captain of Northampton against Birkenhead Park in 1909. If his path was hopelessly blocked he had a ploy known as the punt-pass: he could cross-kick left-footed so accurately that the ball bounced *behind* his opposing left wing and presented Mobbs's right wing with a golden chance to snap up a try.

He was a natural leader. He led his club for six years, scoring 177 tries in all. He led the Barbarians, and he led England (seven caps), and when, on the outbreak of war in 1914, the army wouldn't have him – he was thirty-two and in those early days the generals could afford to pick and choose – Mobbs raised and led his own company of 250 Northampton rugby players and athletes. They marched away in mufti, with Mobbs at their head.

Edgar Mobbs was essentially an Edwardian figure, one of those resolute, hardrunning skippers of the type that John Buchan liked to use as his heroes. His whole career exemplifies the colossal confidence and restless energy that fuelled the First World War. Mobbs – at 32 considered too old for the army in 1914 – raised his own company of sportsmen and led them in France for three years. The cartoon, which appeared in the Northampton Independent, *shows Mobbs winning the war with a good English hand-off while his men advance in columns of four: an image of military thinking which unfortunately was all too close to the truth.*

Vision of E. R. Mobbs and his Corps at the Front.

Mobbs enlisted as a private. Within a month he was a sergeant; within two he was a temporary lieutenant; within a year he was a captain (and not temporary, either). By September 1915 he was Major Mobbs, leading an attack at Loos. A bullet grazed his nose; a nod of the head and Mobbs would have been dead. Instead he went on to become lieutenant-colonel and commander of the battalion that he himself had raised.

In 1916 a shellburst made a mess of his shoulder and sent him to hospital in England, but he was back in France next year with a DSO. On 19 July 1917 the Northamptonshire Regiment had the task of taking an area known as 'Shrewsbury Wood' near Zillebeeke. German machine-gun fire checked the advance. Mobbs led an attack on the gun emplacements and got shot through the neck. He crawled to a shell-hole and found the strength to scribble two reports: one to his HQ and the other to the supporting battery, telling them where to fire. A few minutes later he was dead.

There is a legend that Mobbs used to lead attacks across no-man's land by kicking a rugby ball over the top and then following it up. It may be true but I can find no evidence to support it; Sewell makes no mention of it, and he was not the man to miss a telling detail like that. In any case it doesn't really matter. What matters is that other people *believed* that Mobbs would do it.

For a long time it had seemed that nothing could stop him, but in the end he and his men were just more examples of the sad fact that courage and determination are no match for a well-placed machine-gun post. Nevertheless, his memory endures in the annual Mobbs Memorial match between East Midlands and the Barbarians, at Northampton. Not many players get that sort of treatment. He must have been a hell of a man.

Loose heads and half-wits

It was an old Bridgwater player who first told me about the loose-head craze. He said he could remember matches in Somerset in the 1920s when the scrum crabbed its way clear across the field before they got the ball in. At the time I thought he was exaggerating, but a little research proved that he was not. There was indeed a period when the fight to win the loose head threatened to make the whole game ridiculous. In 1921, E. H. D. Sewell wrote:

> 'Having the loose head is considered of such importance by certain provincial teams that they will go to any lengths to get it. The most usual way is "Run Round". For this a special forward or forwards are detailed to come up at the last moment on the side on which the ball is being put in and thus secure the loose head. At the same time, forwards break away from the far side and come up behind him. If you come up and form outside him and get the loose head, another comes up and forms outside you, and so on. At this stage the game becomes so impossible, that attempting to get the "loose head" is given up by mutual consent "until next time". It could, of course, be stopped by any strong referee, who knew enough about forward play to realise what was going on, but there is no actual rule dealing with it.'

It had been going on for a long time. When the Springboks toured Britain in 1906 their Welsh opponents always contrived to get the loose-head advantage, until the tourists realised what was happening and took steps to counter it. Against Wales they packed down four in the front row. That way, they had the loose head on either side of the scrum. (Presumably Wales persisted with three men up front, which seems very charitable of them.)

The trouble was there was no exact rule covering the situation. For many years the International Board kept insisting that the referee could and should sort out

41

the problem by penalising somebody for obstruction. But the referee didn't, and I can understand why: he was in a very tricky situation. Sewell again:

> 'The loose head nuisance is only in evidence when the referee invariably takes up his position on the Field Side of the scrum – as nearly all referees do – and insists on the ball being put in from that side on every occasion.'

Sewell observed an interesting variation on the theme, which he called 'Opposite Loose Head':

> 'This was practised with great success by a certain Welsh side before the war . . . In this the half secures the ball, and the "loose head" *is openly given up* to the opposing side, but the scrum is formed with all the weight on the far side. The ball is thrown in very fast and hard, and as it leaves the half's hands, *the near side of the scrum gives way and the far side swings forward, receiving the ball as it swings.* Few referees detect this if done as the ball touches the ground, and in any case the operation seems quite legitimate . . . '

The fact is the scrummage law was a mess. As early as 1906 an IB circular had laid down: 'The Referee may order the ball to be put into the scrummage from either side as he may choose.' There was no maximum number of men in the front row: the law merely defined a set scrum as 'formed by one or more players from each side . . . closing up in readiness to allow the ball to be put on the ground between them'. Picture the scene: the scrum goes down and the scrum-half is then told by the referee to put the ball in on the side where his opponents have the loose-head advantage. What would you do?

There was, inevitably, a lot of fighting for the loose head, with the front rows heaving and wrestling to force their heads into new gaps. There was also much Run Round. Sometimes the loose head prop on the non-feeding side wrenched himself clear, dashed around the scrum, and bound himself on to the tight head prop, thus making the former tight head the new hooker (and the old hooker the new tight head on the far side). Sometimes a flanker waited in the offing until the scrum-half was just about to put the ball in, and then nipped forward and added himself as the new loose head. Sometimes both these things happened, so that one team had a *double* loose head. Naturally the other team tried to do the same. The result was farce. Admiral Sir Percy Royds, in his *History of the Laws of Rugby Football*, wrote:

> 'I remember refereeing in a match, Leicester v Cardiff, in which, by this method, two artists at the game caused the scrummage sometimes to travel nearly half-way across the ground before the ball got in properly.'

If Royds couldn't stop the nonsense there had to be something wrong with the laws.

Sewell claimed that there was a rule that 'the ball is not in the scrum properly until it has passed a player on each side', introduced to prevent the loose-head players 'scooping it out of the half's hands, as was done nine years ago'.

Well, yes and no. There was certainly an IB ruling to that effect in 1912, *but it was not included in the laws;* and the poor bloody ref can only go by what his lawbook tells him. Again, in 1921, the IB agreed that the ball must pass a player on each side; again, the RFU did not adopt that change.

The scrum continued to be a headache, a shambles or a joke throughout the 1920s (and indeed it still wasn't right when the Second World War came along). In 1921 the IB added this line to the scrummage law:

> NOTE Loose head is to be dealt with as wilfully preventing under
> this heading.

— which is about as vague and feeble a piece of advice as could be framed; for, as an RFU inquiry reported in 1925, the term 'loose head' was itself undefined, so how was the referee supposed to know what the Note meant? Obviously *some* 'loose head' was perfectly legal, since you couldn't have a scrum without overlapping heads in the front rows. And in any case,

> ' . . . so long as the Referee has power to decide on which side the
> ball must be put into a scrummage so long there will be a struggle
> by the opposing forwards to obtain the outside head on the side
> they expect he will order the ball to be put in.'

The situation was becoming desperate. Already, in 1920, the New Zealand and New South Wales delegates to the IB had proposed 'that the Referee put the ball into the scrummage' in an effort to tidy up the mess. Thank God that proposal died the death. The obvious solution was for the IB to limit the number of front-row players. In 1920 Wales had proposed a maximum of three. Rejected. In 1922 England made the same proposal. Turned down. In 1923 England and Wales tried again, and failed. It wasn't until 1925 that sanity broke through and the IB made a front row of more than three players illegal.

That should have been that; but it wasn't. For some reason the RFU decided to take the sting out of the new law by adding a touch of restraint:

> 'Referees shall not inflict a penalty for this breach of the Law, unless wilful or persistent.'

(This advice survived for at least twenty years; it was still there in 1946.) Certainly the IB didn't notice any immediate improvement. In 1926 it went to the trouble of issuing a press release: 'The Board views with great concern the difficulty which obtains at present in getting the ball fairly into the scrummage', and they blamed the scrum-half for 'irregularities' and the forwards for 'wilfully preventing'. The scramble for the loose head was a long time dying.

Elsewhere in this book I make some comments on the strange capacity of rugby players to louse up a perfectly good game by playing silly-buggers with the laws. To my mind, the era of the loose head squabble (it was too daft to be called a battle) is a classic example. The thought of the Leicester–Cardiff scrum twitching and shuffling thirty or forty yards sideways as the loose head was repeatedly won and lost by the steady arrival of a sort of Elizabethan stage army of forwards who appeared and disappeared and reappeared, while a retired admiral fingered his whistle and wondered how the devil to get the game restarted: that must be one of the great, dotty moments in rugby history.

1893 and all that

The great preservative of Rugby Union football is not Sloane's Liniment. It is Monday morning. As long as the players know they have to go to work on Monday morning, they won't go mad on Saturday afternoon. That is the way the amateur principle works.

It's a matter of priorities. People play Rugby Union for fun, and Rugby League for money. Okay, I know all about boot money and shamateurism, especially in France and Wales, but the fact remains that fewer than one Rugby Union player in ten thousand makes anything at all out of the game, and the rest all pay for their pleasure; while the vast majority of Rugby League players expect to be paid for their efforts, and are.

These expectations have shaped the games. Rugby Union is designed to be fun, to satisfy the players. Rugby League is made to be profitable, to please the spectators. Monday morning is a less potent factor in Rugby League because for its players Saturday afternoon *is* Monday morning. It may be a game (although you could have fooled me, sometimes) but it's primarily a job.

I spell this out so painstakingly because the whole Union–League split has become clouded with charges of snobbery and hypocrisy until the basic truths are often lost in the fog.

God knows it's impossible to do anything in Britain without bringing the class war into it, and God knows people on both sides have done their narrowminded bit to keep that war going. Here are a few grim examples.

In 1929 the president of the RFU, Walter Pearce, when unveiling the Rowland Hill Memorial Gates at Twickenham, referred to 'the Rugby atmosphere – which could only circulate freely among the public-school element of the community'. How Pearce reconciled this with his own humble education at Horfield School, Bristol, beats me. No doubt in 1929 Rugby Union football was a largely middle-class game in England, although not exclusively so: after all, Bob Oakes, president of the RFU in 1933–34, was the son of an army sergeant, born in the militia barracks on the sea front at Hartlepool. And although that year's England XV against Wales (England won at Cardiff, 9-nil) was well studded with Blues and men from the fashionable London clubs, the pack included not only a policeman (John Wright) and a farmer (John Dicks) but also 'Rastus' Longland, a carpenter-and-joiner from Northampton. (What's more the Welsh team, with three Oxbridge men plus one from the Army, one from the RAF, and four from clubs outside the Principality, was far from being pure Valleys stock.)

In any case, the source of most stuffiness was not the players but the officials of the various Rugby Unions. After the Wales–Scotland game in 1931 – a cracker of a match, won by Wales with two tries in the closing minutes – Watcyn Thomas went into the Scots' dressing-room to swap jerseys. He got turfed out by an SRFU official who made it clear that jersey-swapping was the first step on the slippery slope to professionalism. And the attitude of the Welsh Rugby Union was, if anything, worse. Their treatment of George Parsons was so crude as to be paranoid.

Parsons was a Newport lock who had played in the first postwar international against England, in 1947. He was then picked to play against France, in Paris, and he had actually got on to the train with the rest of the team at Newport station when the WRU secretary, Captain Walter Rees, came along and ordered him off. Bleddyn Williams, then the Welsh fly-half, was 'stunned by the harsh treatment served out to Parsons, who was termed to have professionalised himself because it was *alleged* he had been approached by a Rugby League scout'. Parsons was given no chance to defend himself – not that there was anything to defend: the WRU had not accused him of actually doing anything wrong; only of *having been spoken to* by someone who, they had been informed, was a RL scout.

'At that time I hadn't the slightest intention of going North,' Parsons said later. But plenty of RL clubs wanted him, and by its hasty and clumsy behaviour the WRU had tainted his Rugby Union career for ever; so in 1948 he took the money and joined St Helens. It wasn't until 1975 that the WRU relented and awarded Parsons the cap he had won for playing against England. At the same time they presented the former Swansea centre, Idwal Davies, with his cap – withheld since 1939 because Davies too had turned professional after playing for Wales.

But if that sort of vindictiveness has gone, the staunch opposition has not. Rugby Union defines itself as an amateur game. It has no place for anyone who has chosen to play rugby for money, and that's flat. The men of Rugby Union keep the men of Rugby League firmly at arm's length; the longer the arm, the better. In 1975, when a Rugby League World Cup tournament was played on the Swansea ground (which is owned by the city), the Welsh Rugby Union instructed the

Swansea club not to offer the city the use of any of its facilities (tea-rooms or bars, for instance).

Actions like this provoke periodic outbursts of indignation from League supporters. They write furious articles condemning Rugby Hypocrisy and Sporting Apartheid. They deplore the way League players are Shunned Like Lepers By The Old-Boy Networks of Twickenham, the Arms Park and Murrayfield, in the cause of This One-Sided Feud.

What these RL enthusiasts want is the removal of all barriers, so that players can switch and swap between the two codes at will. Curiously, they also seem to have considerable contempt for the other game. Writing in the magazine *Education*, a former RL back, Barry Hugill, reported with enthusiasm the views of the actor and playwright Colin Welland, whom he called 'a RL fanatic'. Welland, he said, foresees a sporting revolution in which RL will sweep the country and supersede RU as a national game. (Fair enough. They can dream, can't they?) But then Hugill – reflecting Welland's views – damns RU as 'long a minority pastime for the elite'. Also a game 'tainted with class prejudice and privilege'. And: 'With the exception of Wales, it is the game for "posh" people, played in the public schools, "better" universities and those maintained schools still resisting comprehensivisation.'

You don't know whether to laugh or cry – especially when Hugill then complains that 'the Rugby Union is conducting a vendetta against ex-professional RL men by refusing to allow them to play Union.'

It's the most extraordinary stew of conflicting claims and attitudes. Welland says RL will sweep the country. Presumably he (and Hugill) believe it is a much better game. Yet they desperately want ex-RL men to be able to play RU – the game for posh people, the tainted game, the game that helps to perpetuate class prejudice. Why, for God's sake? Why make it easier for sturdy, plainspoken, Hovis-eating RL men to be corrupted by degenerate, class-ridden, vodka-tonic RU clubs? Why not urge them to stay with RL? Why bother with second best?

I suppose a few facts ought to come into the argument somewhere. Quoting facts is not so much fun as waging the class war, but here goes anyway. In England, over two thousand schools belong to the Rugby Football Schools Union. Fewer than two hundred are fee-paying schools; the vast majority are comprehensives. More than a quarter of a million people play RU each week in England, the vast majority outside the Home Counties. I took the trouble to analyse a recent England squad of twenty-five international players. Seven lived in the north, five in the midlands, four in the west, three in Wales, two were at Cambridge and only two lived in London. There were four students, five teachers, three sales reps, a farmer, a clerk, a fruit-and-veg merchant, a printer, a site manager, a trainee, a factory worker, an instructor, a restaurant owner, a police constable, an insurance broker, a sales executive, and a bricklayer (unemployed at the time).

So much for posh.

That, of course, doesn't answer the question of why there should be any barriers between the two games, or why RU sticks so doggedly to its principle of amateurism. The answer, as I said at the start, is Monday morning; but to appreciate the full significance of Monday morning it's necessary to know a bit of history. For the really big year in rugby was not 1823, when William Webb Ellis probably didn't do anything worth writing home about, but 1893, when the men in charge of the RFU made a most difficult, courageous and important decision. It was also to be a thoroughly misunderstood decision and one for which they took a lot of stick, but that's life; and their reward is the fact that nearly a century later the game they defended is alive and well and being played in almost every country in the world.

It didn't look like that in 1893. It looked to many people as if the Rugby Football Union had committed ritual suicide.

What you have to bear in mind is that, in the early years, rugby was a bigger game in the north of England than it was in the south. They were playing county matches between Yorkshire and Lancashire before Scotland challenged England to the first international contest. B. Fletcher Robinson made a survey of the state of rugby in 1896, and he emphasised that it was, 'in the North especially the great pastime of the labouring man'. Northerners had made their mark in the England team: 'For many years Yorkshire and Lancashire have produced the finest players, and, what is still more important, the most honourable sportsmen in England.' One such was Horace Duckett of Bradford, who played half-back for England and for Yorkshire. In those days the match between Yorkshire and the Rest of England served as an England trial; in Duckett's time Yorkshire won it three years out of four.

The England XX that met the Scotland XX in 1871 had seven northerners – four from Manchester, three from Liverpool; and throughout the 1870s and 1880s it was unusual to see an England team with fewer than half a dozen men from clubs like Preston Grasshoppers, Bradford, Hull, Manchester Rangers, Birkenhead Park, Leeds, Swinton, Halifax, Wakefield Trinity, Heckmondwike, Salford, Wigan, Tadcaster, Oldham and Batley. When England beat the touring New Zealand Natives (mistakenly called the Maoris) in 1889, eleven of the team were northerners, including the captain, Fred Bonsor of Bradford. In 1891, nine northerners helped England beat Wales at Newport and then Ireland in Dublin.

The next year there were eleven players from the north when England beat them both again, at home; and the number rose to thirteen for the match against Scotland in Edinburgh – another England victory.

But the very strength of rugby in the north was creating problems. It had become big business. When B. Fletcher Robinson set about describing what he called *A Modern Game of Rugby Football* he chose a visit by Cambridge University to a Yorkshire mill town. The students, who included three England caps as well as big men from Scotland and Wales, were impressed by the scene that met them when they went on to the field of play:

> 'There we stand, the gladiators of the ninteenth-century colosseum. The great multitude wraps us round with its dark embrace; a silent crowd, some twenty thousand strong, rising tier on tier above us. There is something so businesslike in the concentrated stare of those forty thousand eyes, that an ancient Roman, could he be placed amongst them, would probably express surprise that we did not turn to the central stand and cry the "Morituri te

salutant" to the committee. A young undergraduate, who has never played in the North before, turns to me, half in jest and half in earnest, and says, "I don't like this, old chap; I feel as if I couldn't run away!" I tell him that I quite agree with him. But our talk is interrupted by a mighty shout that goes echoing away into the distance. What is it? – ah, the "home" team. Conscious of their popularity, the men come skipping and jumping on to the field, throwing the ball they bring with them from one to the other, and playing the practical jokes which are the average Englishman's idea of humour. Fifteen strong, square fellows, hard as nails all of them; short and dark for the most part, such as the Yorkshire towns breed – a race apart from their tall, fair, broad-shouldered brethren of the dales. Three of them, indeed, are of the latter class, immense towers of muscle and brawn, but they are the exception, and quite dwarf their sturdy companions.'

It turns out to be a fullblooded game. At one point a Yorkshireman almost breaks away:

'But, see, speeding across the ground comes our Scotchman; two of their men are close together. Surely, if the first is tackled, it will avail us little, for he is already preparing to pass the ball to his companion. But no; at his topmost speed – and he has weight as well to back him – the Scotchman takes them both, an arm for each, and over go the three in a struggling heap . . . '

In the end the Cambridge team narrowly wins – by a goal to a try. But what is interesting is the role of the spectators. At a line-out,

'An incident occurs which raises the wildest enthusiasm among the crowding masses . . . One of the visitors catches the ball, but he is hurled to the ground by his gigantic opponent with quite unnecessary violence. The crowd cheer loudly. You must not be surprised at that. Remember, please, that half of them have come in the hope of seeing a bit of "scrappin'" ' . . . '

In the north, the size of the crowd (and therefore of the gate) had begun to influence the game. The clubs made a lot of money; the players were ordinary working men who lost half a day's pay or more whenever they turned out, and they might turn out two or even three times a week; so it was only natural for the club to wish to compensate them by making up the lost wages. Nobody in the north felt there was anything wrong in this. On the contrary they considered it simple justice. They believed they were doing the game a service by negating a disability that would otherwise have deprived a club of a good player. After all, the man wasn't getting paid for playing; he was getting compensated for what was called 'broken time'. Not the same thing at all. Except, of course, in the eyes of the RFU.

Everyone in the north knew that these 'broken-time payments' were against the rules. They thought the rules were stupid and so they broke them cheerfully – but quietly. In the 1880s and early 1890s there was widespread professionalism but it was veiled professionalism. The feeling in the north was that it was all very well for well-to-do southerners: they could afford the luxury of total amateurism. Conditions were a lot harder in the north. What good did absolute amateurism do rugby if it kept half the players out of the game?

That analysis was all very well as far as it went. The trouble was the reality went a lot further.

When a club gave money to half the team, the other half sometimes wondered aloud why they were being treated differently. The answer – that they were not losing wages – might not satisfy them. Similarly, when players discovered that some clubs were also paying expenses (and why not? Why penalise a player simply because his travel costs were heavy?) it was not long before the practice spread. And it wasn't long after that before some clubs developed reputations for being very generous indeed with their expenses – which could be an added attraction to a player who was thinking of making a move.

What began as a means of preventing hardship developed easily into a way of avoiding dissatisfaction, and from that it was a short step to using the money to stimulate or even to reward. Performance and payment came to be naturally associated with each other, whether the player asked for the money or not.

One man – a famous international who played for a Yorkshire club – made it very clear that he vigorously opposed professionalism, but all the same he played so brilliantly one afternoon that when he reached the dressing-room he found that a collection of £2 14s 8d had been placed in his boots. It was easy to start payment; less easy to check it. By the early 1890s it was an open secret that northern clubs were spending money to recruit players who then got a regular wage, perhaps with a bonus when they played well. And the players, conscious of the fact that they were paid out of gate money, knew how important it was to please the crowd. The tail was beginning to wag the dog.

There were other differences of opinion between north and south, in particular over the question of league competitions, but the big problem was broken time. Many northerners disliked the sham. They were not ashamed of what their clubs were doing, and so the pretence that it wasn't happening annoyed them. In 1893 they decided to bring the theory into line with the facts. They decided to alter the RFU's rules of amateurism.

If they had kept quiet and sprung the idea on the RFU without warning they might well have succeeded: there were a lot of votes in the north. As it was, the RFU committee got wind of the proposal and had time to drum up opposition to it. More to the point, they had time to plan a counter-attack. One of the committee's honorary secretaries, H. E. Steed, called on those clubs who did not expect to send representatives to the general meeting. He persuaded them to vote by proxy. By the time Steed had finished he had 120 proxies in his pocket.

The general meeting of the RFU was held at the Westminster Palace Hotel on 20 September 1893. There was a record attendance. In the chair was the president

who – to add a nice touch to the drama – was himself a northerner. William Cail was a manufacturer and export merchant. His club was Newcastle Northern. Seven years earlier, he had been largely responsible for revising the laws. This was his second term as president, and he had been a member of the International Board since 1890. (He stayed on the IB until 1925.) Cail carried a lot of weight in the world of rugby.

What he presided over at that meeting was a brilliant little counter-insurgency operation, planned and carried out by the Establishment. It was all thoroughly legal, all quite correct and proper. But this very propriety made it all the more intolerable to the losers. They got beaten fair and square, there was no room for compromise, and the only courses left open to them were submission or secession.

The operation was all over quite quickly. Two Yorkshiremen, J. A. Miller and M. Newsome, both members of the Rugby Union committee, proposed and seconded:

> 'That players be allowed compensation for *bona fide* loss of time.'

This proposal was never put to the vote. The honorary secretary of the Union, G. Rowland Hill, moved an amendment:

> 'That this meeting, believing that the above principle is contrary to
> the true interest of the game and its spirit, declines to sanction the
> same.'

R. S. Whalley, a vice-president (and from Lancashire), seconded it. The meeting voted. 136 opposed the amendment but 282 supported it. Broken time was rejected. It was a crucial decision. 'The majority greeted its announcement by a tumult of applause,' wrote O. L. Owen in his *History of the RFU*. 'The minority mostly sat in grim silence. It was very much like a declaration of war.'

It had been a damned close-run thing, too. Although 481 clubs belonged to the RFU, the total of votes cast was only 418. Which clubs did not take part? It would be interesting to know. If they were remote from London – which seems a fair guess – then they might have tended to support broken time. A majority of 146 for the amendment looks comfortable enough, but take away Steed's proxies and the majority shrinks to only 26. Suppose there had been no Steed; suppose instead that Miller and Newsome had done some proxy-hunting of their own: the amendment might well have been lost, the proposal won, and England would have woken up on 21 September 1893 to discover that, from now on, money was no obstacle to amateurism, amateurism no obstacle to money, and the dividing line between the two had gone forever.

Yorkshire v England, 1889. Four years later the bowler hats almost changed the course of English rugby: M. Newsome and J. A. Miller (president and secretary of Yorkshire) proposed to allow broken-time payment and were defeated by only 26 votes – if you don't count the proxies.

The Union was jolted into swift action. Another general meeting changed the by-laws in a kind of pre-emptive strike against any subversive activity from the north. The first by-law now declared that 'only clubs composed entirely of amateurs' could belong to the Union, whose headquarters 'shall be in London where all general meetings shall be held'. That was calculated to make life difficult for the dissidents; meanwhile the Union drew up complete and cast-iron laws against professionalism in any shape, form or fashion. These laws came into force on 19 September 1895; but by then the big split had already happened.

Twenty of the leading clubs in Yorkshire and Lancashire left to form their own association: the Northern Union. Others followed. Before the vote on broken time, 481 clubs were members of the RFU. By 1896 the number was down to 383. By 1903 it was 244, and the prolonged exodus left English rugby struggling to survive. In the ten years before the vote, England had won the Triple Crown three times and shared it twice; in the sixteen years after the vote, England never once won the title. The loss of the north had been a great sacrifice.

And all for what? Precious little, according to the critics of the RFU. They said that the stuffed shirts, by their snobbish mistreatment of working men less privileged than themselves, had crippled the game they claimed to defend. It is a view that persists to this day. A recent potted-history of Rugby League begins:

> 'Rugby League arrived because the administrators of the Rugby Union refused to believe that there existed men in this country who could not afford to take time off work to play football. Agitation for broken-time expenses among the clubs of the mill and mining towns of Yorkshire and Lancashire was met with frosty incomprehension – then curt refusal – by the Rugby Union.'

It would be stupid to claim that snobbery played no part in the debate over broken time: in late-Victorian England, class-consciousness was part of the air that everyone breathed. But to say that the administrators of the RFU didn't know the facts of industrial life in the north is to indulge in a kind of inverted snobbery. The truth is they knew very well that men working a six-day week suffered some hardship when they took time off to play football. (It's not as if the RFU was run exclusively by southerners: as we've seen, in 1893 both the president, Cail, and a vice-president, Whalley, were from the north.) Perhaps some of the clubs in the south didn't fully realise what a difference broken time made in the north; perhaps they didn't altogether appreciate the real difficulties of fielding a team made up of mill-workers, miners or labourers. But the men who voted against broken time were far from frostily incomprehensive of developments in the north. They comprehended only too well that unless the line between amateurism and professionalism was drawn clearly and held firmly, it would start to crumble. Any attempts to bend it here or twist it there would threaten its entire existence. You could no more bend the amateur line than you could bend the off-side line.

But it was difficult to appreciate the importance of this when all that seemed to be at stake was the handing out of a few shillings by clubs who could well afford it to men who certainly needed it. Indeed, when the Northern Union was formed the most that any player was allowed, to replace lost wages, was six shillings a day. The players still regarded themselves as amateurs. The northern clubs had no intention of playing anything except the game they had always played. They had not left the RFU in order to *change* rugby but in order to *preserve* it, in the only way they saw open to them. They loved the game. They had its best interests at heart. Yet in a few years they had completely changed it.

They began by changing the laws of the game in order to make play more attractive to the spectator. In 1897 they reduced the points value of kicked goals, scrapped the line-out and made the scrum-half stay behind the scrummage instead of being free to harry his opposite number. In 1899 they changed the tackle law so that the tackled player no longer had to release the ball. The principle of 'possession' had arrived. The idea was to limit stoppages by letting the tackled player pass back to a team-mate; the effect was to enable one team to keep the ball despite repeatedly being tackled. In 1901 the knock-on law was relaxed to give the player a second bite at the cherry, and the need to attract bigger crowds led the twelve strongest clubs to set up the Challenge Cup competition. In 1904 the scrummage law was modified to stop wheeling. And – the crucial change – in 1906 teams were cut to thirteen men. All these alterations had the same aim: to brighten up the game. If a match were scrappy or dull, with too much barging or mauling, it must be the fault of the laws. And the game could not afford to be anything but bright: quite literally could not afford it. The six-shilling limit had long since gone.

Thus only ten years after the Northern Union was formed, all the distinctive features of Rugby League football had arrived. With hindsight it's plain that the changes were inevitable. Once the players were paid, the demands of the spectators became at least as important as those of the teams. That meant the clubs had to regard themselves as part of the entertainment industry. If they couldn't pull the crowds through the turnstiles then they would go out of business just as surely as any music hall that failed to put bums on seats. The perpetual problem of Rugby League is that it is always looking over its shoulder at the terraces, wondering and worrying about the size of the gate. And the paradox is that Rugby League, by constantly tinkering with its game to please the crowd, has never produced a spectacle half as exciting as the game of Rugby Union, which is primarily interested in giving the player what he wants.

But if Rugby League has always been the poor relation, why does Rugby Union insist on cold-shouldering it? What is there to be afraid of?

The answer is that Rugby Union has no reason to be afraid of Rugby League but it has no cause to befriend it, either. Throughout its history, Rugby League has found many of its best players in the ranks of RU. These men have benefited from years of training and coaching and encouragement, and their clubs are entitled to feel bitter when they are lost to the appeal of RL chequebooks. It might seem uncharitable for a RU club to ban from its clubhouse all RL men, including former members of the club; but what is the alternative? Should the club let them stroll through the bar, recruiting the cream of the 1st XV? That would be carrying charity to the point of folly – especially when RL keeps making strenuous efforts to move into RU territory, and even to take over RU grounds.

The main target has been South Wales. Four separate attempts have been made to establish RL there.

The first was in 1907. The Northern Union set up teams in Aberdare, Ebbw

Vale and Merthyr; next year there was professional rugby at Barry, Treherbert and Mid Rhondda too. It didn't work. There were booster tours by New Zealand and Australian RL sides but too few people came to watch and the NU clubs faded away.

The Northern Union changed its name to the Rugby League in 1922, and tried again. This time the invasion got as far as Llanelli. A RL syndicate rented the Stebonheath ground in 1926, but the venture collapsed within a few months. RL continued to flicker into the 1930s – some professional internationals were played at Llanelli and Pontypridd – but again it failed to win an audience.

The Second World War came and went, and the RL crusaders made a third attempt. They set up teams in Ebbw Vale, Llanelli, Barry and Cardiff. They even penetrated Bridgend and took the Brewery Field ground from Bridgend RFC (who didn't get it back until 1957). By 1950 a league of eight RL teams was operating in Wales. Neath and Abertillery were two strongpoints from which RL planned to expand. 'Cohorts are to go out into every town and village in Wales preaching the League game . . . ' said a RL spokesman, 'in an honest endeavour to raise the standard of rugby football in South Wales and regain some of the past glories of the game . . . Nothing will prevent us . . . even if it takes up to fifteen years, we are coming into Wales.' They came, but the big crowds did not. On average, about a thousand people paid to watch a match, and that wasn't nearly enough to meet the payroll. Towards the end, Cardiff RL were often playing in front of only a hundred spectators.

The fourth attempt was launched in the late 1970s, and although it hasn't been a total flop, it hasn't been the triumph that the pre-launch publicity claimed for it. This is odd. Even with all the added advantages of television coverage, sponsorship, Sunday matches, floodlights, and the affluence and mobility of a car-owning public, RL still refuses to catch fire in the south (and many RL clubs are going broke in the north). Why?

There are, I think, four main reasons.

One is the shortage of brilliant players. RL can always buy top talent from RU, but often that talent is past its prime when it signs the contract. Crowds will not flock to see *old* international stars. Which raises the question: why don't the top RU players go over to RL sooner?

The answer to that is also the second reason for RL's problems. RL simply isn't such a good game to play. It's hard, it's sometimes brutal, and there is far more sheer bruising collision than you get in RU, but above all it's very limited. Many of the people who go to watch rugby in the south have played RU, and to them the sight of a man *deliberately accepting the tackle so that he can die with the ball* is like a confession of failure. They want to see him *beat* his opponent, not run into the man; and if he can't make a break then let him pass, and keep the attack going. God knows there are boring RU matches too, but when it's played well – with the ball flickering through many pairs of hands and fresh patterns of play being spontaneously shaped as the whole team strives to create the gap that means success – RU offers a richness and an excitement that makes RL look very predictable. Indeed it *is* predictable. Its obsession with possession has turned it into a series of bulldozing charges. The game goes in fits and stops.

J. J. Williams (Llanelli, Wales, Lions, and one of the best postwar wing-threequarters in the world) described the difference:

> 'It's a hell of a tough game, League. I mean, they don't care, you know? If you've done a bit in the first half, scored one or two, at half-time their coach will say to the bloke who's marking you, "Right, I want Williams out. I don't care how you do it, but get him off." I don't mind a hard game, but I don't want that sort of rugby.
>
> 'To me it's an uninteresting game at the best, Rugby League. There's no intellectual satisfaction. Rugby Union now, you have to think all the time, both as a player and a spectator. Rugby League, and soccer the same, they're too simple. Anyone can understand them . . . I love Rugby Union, I love the game: Rugby League is nothing beside it.'

J. J. Williams turned down an offer of £15,000 to play Rugby League. (That was in 1975, when £15,000 was worth £30,000 or £40,000 in 1980s money.) In 1962, Australian and New Zealand Rugby League clubs tried to buy Colin Meads and Kel Tremain for $15,000 and $10,000 respectively; both refused. Some good players have turned professional and liked it: David Watkins (Newport, Wales, Lions) went north and became an equally great success at the League game. Chico Hopkins (Maesteg and Wales) went north and, often as not, couldn't keep a first-team place. Nor could he go back to RU. Money doesn't always buy happiness.

Not that RL is a big-money sport. Certainly, a top RU player may get ten or twenty thousand pounds as his signing-on fee, but the average RL player doesn't make his fortune on the field. When Adrian Alexander left the Harlequins and went to Oldham for £15,000 he joined a team that was paid £50 a man for a win or £15 for a defeat (1979 figures). Clubs working on that sort of budget are not likely to generate supreme technical expertise and brilliant ballyhoo on the

J. J. Williams (Wales and Lions) looking askance at offers to turn professional: 'I don't mind a hard game, but I don't want that sort of rugby.'

scale that has made gridiron football such a colossal and lucrative spectacle in the USA.

Yet, at the same time, the very fact that the players *are* being paid takes something away from the contest. There is a vigorous local patriotism in the support for RU club games, and it is partly inspired by the knowledge that everyone on the field is there for love and not for money. Of course there is skill and courage and teamwork in RL too; but every spectator knows that high on the RL player's list of priorities is the matter of gain: he wouldn't be out there if he weren't being paid. And while there is nothing dishonourable about playing a game for money, it's not the same as playing it for its own sake. The motives in RU are unmixed, and this generates a purer enthusiasm. It is a curious truth that, even in this commercial age (or perhaps because of it), men will do more for love than for money.

A recent television documentary followed the fortunes of a struggling RL club. Badly beaten in the first half of a match, the team found the chairman – a local businessman – waiting in the dressing-room at half-time. He made a stirring, Dunkirk-type speech that didn't seem to have much effect. Then he said: 'And if it's motivation you want, here's two hundred extra bonus for winning'. He tossed a wad of notes on to a table. They sat and looked at it as if it was an old sock.

Thirteen into two hundred is £15.38. They went back out and lost. I had the feeling that the chairman's offer had actually *discouraged* them. It was as if he had put a cash price on their missing pride: £15.38. It's not much. It wasn't enough.

RL keeps tinkering with its rules in the hope of bringing about 'the revolution we have been waiting for', in the words of a former chairman of the RL Council. He was talking about the abolition of the scrum after the sixth tackle. This takes RL another step closer to American football, where a team that is unsuccessful in its four 'downs' concedes possession to its opponents. American football is played in four quarters of fifteen minutes each, and it's significant that RL, when it tried to get established in the USA, agreed to restructure its game into four quarters; this was to make room for television commercials.

America, however, has shown no great interest in RL. The curious thing is that the game Americans have taken up in a big way is RU. With their passion for crunching tackles and their ability to turn almost anything into business, Americans might have been expected to prefer RL; instead they have chosen the amateur game. In 1960 there were about fifty RU clubs in the US. By 1980 there were nearly a thousand. In the 1960s British clubs made missionary tours to the USA and invariably they won. By 1977 the newly formed USA RFU was sending its national team on tour to England, and the Eagles were not disgraced when they played a strong England XV at Twickenham.

This is a remarkable demonstration of the simple yet powerful appeal of amateur rugby. What attracts the young Americans who have taken it up in their tens of thousands is the very fact that the game is *not* played for money. Everything else in life is business. It's all organised to make money. The yardstick of success is profit. Amateur rugby is different. It has only one purpose and only one justification: to be played for fun. In the last twenty years, young Americans – often reacting against the grim mechanisation of college gridiron football – have discovered that the game is for the players. In a world where every other sport is sponsored, promoted, organised, televised and generally put through the pressure cooker of commerce, RU is different. That's why all those Americans like it: not because it tries to beat other sports at their game but because it goes its own way and offers its own, separate satisfactions.

There is a lesson to be learned from this on the other side of the Atlantic. The lesson is: leave well alone.

That, I realise, is not a fashionable plea. All the fashionable talk nowadays is of the need for change.

When Adrian Alexander left the Harlequins, he said: 'The Union game, as we know it, is dying in England. The players are fed up with all the old men clinging to their bit of power. It's the last bastion of amateurism, really, yet there is so much hypocrisy. I've never earned a penny out of Rugby Union but I was on a tour four or five years ago with a Welsh player who admitted he was on £50 a match then.'

The former All Blacks captain, Graham Mourie, raised the question of the players' need 'for some form of financial compensation' in his 1982 autobiography:

> 'They cannot continue to make themselves available for an increasing number of tours while at the same time their incomes are either reduced or stopped completely. The burden on players' wives, financial and otherwise, is unfair and often intolerable. I devised a system by which players who could show hardship could be compensated for the time they are away on tour, and suggested the payment of the average weekly wage, as fixed by the Statistics Department, as a useful starting point. The question of who would pay and who would be paid is not as complex as some administrators might believe, nor would it be the thin end of the wedge that could hold ajar the door of professionalism. Our intention is to retain the amateur status of the game because the game would founder without it. The important thing to digest is that the players are not wanting to be paid for playing. They simply do not want the economic base of their lives to be eroded while they are playing.'

After the 1971 British Lions' tour to New Zealand, their coach, Carwyn James, said:

> ' . . . the day may come when something has to be done about players who spend time away from work because of rugby . . . The fact is that employers are being highly generous. They are subsidising the players, and the game as well, by not docking wages and salaries. I want the game to remain amateur but we are not living in a world where players are well-off enough to forgo their salaries . . . And youngsters can have a hard time of it. Don't forget these tours can make up to half a million profit.'

When the journalist he was talking to (Roy McKelvie of *The Guardian*) suggested that the Unions might reimburse the employers for the money they paid out to players involved in representative rugby, James said: 'What a brilliant idea.'

More recently (September 1983) Clem Thomas, a former captain of Wales, has written:

> 'There is an urgent need to restructure the game's administration and, without being irresponsible, the regulations on amateurism could be relaxed to allow the players space to breathe. I believe a clear affirmation should be made of the principles and ethos of the game and consideration given to a charter which would be more in line with modern thinking.
>
> The charter should state that:
>
> 1. When a player retires he should be allowed to write or broadcast on the game for money without forfeiting his amateur status.
>
> 2. If a player, because of his standing in the game, is asked to indulge in a commercial activity (opening a store or advertising a product, for example) he should be allowed to receive payment without endangering his amateur status.'

Now that is an impressive line-up. Alexander captained the Harlequins, Mourie led the All Blacks, James coached the Lions and Thomas, in addition to his rugby credentials, writes for *The Observer*. They all say that RU football should change its basic rules of amateurism. I say they are wrong.

Alexander's sneers are not surprising; in his position, he would say that sort of thing, wouldn't he? (The facts are that the Union game in England shows no signs of dying: in the five years since he wrote it off, it has grown steadily by ten or a dozen new clubs a year. And as for 'old men clinging to their bit of power': it's a democratic game, and if the clubs don't like what their representatives do at Twickenham they can elect someone else.) Alexander's complaint of hypocrisy is a familiar one, and there can be no doubt that some players are surreptitiously paid; but it's not at all clear what Alexander's alternative would be. Which would he eliminate: the hypocrisy or the amateurism? And how would he do it? We don't know. This is true of so many whingeing players. Their remarks tend to be negative. They complain about the present set-up but they make no effort to describe a better one.

Graham Mourie has at least done some homework. His proposal contains three significant points. The first is his reference to 'a system by which players who could show hardship could be compensated'. The second is his insistence that 'the players do not want to be paid for playing'. The third is his claimed intention 'to retain the amateur status of the game'.

We have been here before, in 1893. Mourie's proposal is the old broken-time argument all over again, with the difference that he has expanded a half-day's pay to a week's wages. Like Mourie, the northern clubs began making broken-time payments with the best of possible intentions. They too were convinced that they were preserving the amateur status of the game. They were preventing hardship, that's all. The last thing their players wanted was to be paid for playing. Yet the last thing they wanted was almost the first thing they got, and within a dozen years the Northern Union was ruled by professionalism. I have no doubt that Mourie's system would go the same way. The need to 'show hardship' would soon be scrapped: players – especially tourists – dislike any kind of internal discrimination or special treatment, and quite rapidly everyone would be getting the same average weekly wage – until some of the players (or more likely their wives) pointed out that they normally earn *twice* the average wage, and so to avoid hardship each man should be paid not less than what he would have made anyway. That, of course, could be quite a lot. He might be a doctor, or a lawyer, or (God help us) a gung-ho self-employed insurance salesman making more money than he can count. Never mind, the game can afford it – look at the gate receipts! Always bearing in mind, too, that the insurance salesman is also a brilliant fly-half (Barry John crossed with Jackie Kyle plus a hint of Richard Sharp and a touch of Gordon Waddell) whose very name will draw truly enormous crowds, so obviously he's worth every thousand he's paid. Well, not exactly *paid*. You can't say he's *paid*. I mean, the Inland Revenue reckons he's paid, so he's got to pay tax on the income, but really the man's an amateur, he *enjoys* playing. Of course, if we didn't pay him – sorry, sorry: compensate him – he wouldn't play, and that would be a terrible loss to the gate. What? Did I say 'gate'? Sorry, sorry: I meant 'game'. Terrible loss to the game. Same thing, really.

What is remarkable about Mourie is the way he manages to support these warring ideas with no apparent sense of strain. Carwyn James had the same curious facility. He could say *I want the game to remain amateur* and then add *but we are not living in a world where players are well-off enough to forgo their salaries.* . . . It is as if, by uttering the creed (part one) he had made any other statement (part two) acceptable. But the inevitable implication of part two is that players cannot and should not forgo their salaries. The game should pay the players: that is what James meant. The rest – all his remarks about generous employers subsidising the game, and about youngsters having a hard time of it, and about tours making big profits – is irrelevant. It is irrelevant because none of it is new. It was all there in 1893. Indeed, some of it was more true then than now.

As the standard of living has gone up, so the average player is now *more* able to afford time off to play rugby, not less. For instance, the idea that fewer men these days can afford to go on a Lions tour is pure myth. The 1938 Lions travelled to South Africa by sea; the journey out and back added two months to the tour. Three of the finest backs in Britain – Cliff Jones, Wilf Wooller and Wilson Shaw – had to decline the invitation. Vivian Jenkins went. The tourists got three shillings a day pocketmoney, worth perhaps £1 now; but each man was asked to bring £50 to cover his incidental expenses: the equivalent of at least £500 today. Jenkins managed this only through the kindness of his friends. Each player also took his own evening dress – white tie and tails. Today's Lions (who are given a full set of clothes before they go and who get an expenses allowance of £12 a day or more) are spared that sort of thing.

But even supposing this were not the case, so what? If a man decides that he cannot afford to go on tour, that is no indictment of amateurism. It's his choice. He may believe it's more important to sit examinations or start a new job or bring in the harvest. If such aims or ambitions matter more to him than rugby, that may be a matter of unhappiness to the selectors but it's no reason to persuade him otherwise with money. He may have a wife and three kids to feed, or heavy hire-purchase payments on his new Jag to keep up, or crippling gambling debts to pay. Tough luck. When he declares that he can't afford to take time off work to go on tour it may seem terribly unfair, but what has that to do with the case? He knew what he was getting into when he married, or bought the Jag, or took up baccarat and chemin-de-fer.

Two fallacies underlie most of the mutterings of discontent about rugby's insistence on an amateur status.

One is the belief that this insistence is fundamentally unfair, and that fairness can be redistributed along with a certain amount of money. The truth is that complete and universal fairness is a mirage and those who go hunting it are doomed to disappointment. Life is unfair. It is manifestly unfair that I should be too short to be a Lions lock, too slow to be a Lions wing, and too clumsy to be a Lions fly-half; but that's life. It is also manifestly unfair that (say) a policeman, or a doctor, or a long-distance truck-driver, should fail to reach his rugby potential because shift-work gets in the way of training and playing; but that too is life. Equally it is manifestly unfair that some players should be unable to afford to stop work and go on tour; but the simpleminded solution – make up their lost income – would create a far greater unfairness than it would remove. The amateur principle would be seen to be breached, and thereafter it would be a hundred times more difficult to resist creeping shamateurism, semi-professionalism, inflated payment of expenses and so on. If Lions tourists can get a wage, why not (for instance) let the Welsh Rugby Union pay the Welsh team when they go on tour? And if that is allowed, why not let a club pay some or all of its players when they tour? And then keep up the habit when they come back? Plus, say, a bonus for winning?

The second fallacy is the belief that amateurism goes out of the window when big profits come in at the door. 'The top players' efforts and brilliance are bringing millions into the game,' goes the argument, 'so it's high time the top players got their share.'

If, indeed, there is a great lake of loot spilling over, then I suggest that the top players would not qualify for first place in the queue to lap it up. International rugby matches don't just happen: they are the result of a lot of unpaid work by men elected to the various Rugby Unions. What's more, the whole complex structure of the game depends on the unsung efforts of many other amateurs working at many different levels: schoolboy, youth, student, under-23, national 'B' team. Furthermore, each level depends on other men who are prepared to devote large chunks of their time to such essential services as coaching, selection, refereeing, disciplinary committees, and making sure there's a properly blown-up ball available at kick-off time. (I have known games where this last requirement had been overlooked. The importance of good organisation suddenly loomed large, believe me.)

Of course, the top players are important too. But the only way they got to the top was on the willing backs of an army of people who helped them there. *That's* where the money should go, back to the grassroots; and that (by and large) is where it *does* go. Most Unions face huge bills for maintaining or rebuilding their stadiums. Apart from that expense, they spend their income on the players: all the players. There is a lot more to rugby than international matches, and the idea that top players should get a piece of the action just because it exists is absurd.

There is still Clem Thomas's claim to be considered.

He wants a new charter, one that would let a *retired* player write or broadcast about the game for money, and would let an *active* player exploit his status as a rugby celebrity for commercial gain, in each case without loss of amateur status.

The first suggestion makes some sense. The second makes none. Let's get the second out of the way first.

Its weakness is revealed by Thomas's curious choice of words. He talks of a player being 'asked to indulge in a commercial activity' and then being 'allowed to receive payment'. He makes the deal sound awfully casual ('*Do us a favour, Gareth, nip round the corner and open our new supermarket for us, boyo*') and he makes the reward sound almost accidental ('*Good morning, Gareth, the manager asked me to give you this box of groceries, and thank you very much. I hope you like Spam?').* Perhaps it sometimes happens like that, and no harm done; but I have spent many years in advertising and sales promotion, and in my experience it is not an area where people 'indulge in commercial activities'. It's a much more serious business than that. It's run by professionals, and they expect the people whom they pay to act with equal professionalism, on the basis of contracts that state fees, services and conditions. The company is exploiting the celebrity's popularity in order to boost its business. The celebrity understands this and is prepared to work hard in order to justify the hefty fee that he – or more likely his agent – has negotiated. We are not talking here about free boxes of groceries. We are talking about big money. When an advertiser can easily spend £50,000 for one network television commercial in prime time, he is quite prepared to offer that sort of money (or double it) to a celebrity whose face will, he thinks, enhance the impact of his advertising.

Without even trying, I can think of a dozen players who, at the height of their careers, could have earned a fortune from advertising or sponsorships. Their rugby fame was such that they could have stopped working and done nothing but practise, train and play, thus making sure they stayed rich and famous.

That is not what the game is all about.

By contrast, Clem Thomas's first proposal makes a lot of sense. Rugby Union's staunch defence of the amateur principle has been mainly for the protection of the player. It is hard to see how the game could be damaged by allowing an ex-player who writes or broadcasts about it, to keep his amateur status and therefore be available to serve it as a coach, adviser or committeeman. As things stand, it is very easy to see how the game suffers from losing the services of a Bill Beaumont, a Phil Bennett, a Graham Mourie, or an Ian McLauchlan.

In fact the change has already been half-made.

In 1960, Ireland learned – with a shock that spilled a thousand jars of Guinness – that Andy Mulligan was out of the team, apparently for ever. Mulligan had been the Irish scrum-half since 1956, when he was still at Cambridge, partnering first Jacky Kyle and then Mike English. From the start he was obviously Lions calibre. The fresh-faced, schoolboyish charm and the slim build were deceptive: he was clever and he was tough. He had the true scrum-half's outlook: to take whatever came and make the most of it. Mulligan took rubbish and made it into half-chances. He took chances and made them into tries. Above all he had an endless zest for the game that infected others. Plug Mulligan into a team and it lit up.

So why drop him? Answer: because he had become a journalist and one of the things he wrote about was rugby. Law 19 of the Irish RFU said that players or committeemen must not write about rugby for reward. Goodbye, Andrew

Mulligan . . . or so it seemed. Then there was a rapid reappraisal of the situation, and Mulligan was back in the team. An exception to Law 19 had been made for those who were solely engaged in journalism (which includes broadcasting).

That's how things stand. It means that I, as a full-time writer, can do television commentary on rugby without disqualifying myself from belonging to a referees' society; indeed for many years I reffed midweek and worked in the press box on Saturdays. I have written books on rugby for gain and at the same time served on advisory committees at Twickenham. All this is perfectly legal and respectable. Yet if the ex-captain of England writes or speaks a word about rugby and gets paid for it he disqualifies himself permanently from serving Twickenham, his club, his county or indeed any part of the world of RU, in any way whatsoever.

Now that is daft. If Twickenham can find a use for a broken-down hack like me, it can certainly benefit from the experience of a man who knows what it's like to be out there in the thick of the action. And if Don Rutherford, the RFU's Technical

The traditional rewards of rugby: Clem Thomas with the match ball stuffed up his jersey joins hands in the singing of 'Now is the Hour' after the Barbarians–All Blacks match, 1954.

Administrator (a coded signal concealing the job of coaching organiser) and Ray Williams, who used to be his opposite number in Wales, could write books on the game without bringing about the end of Western civilisation as we know it, it becomes increasingly difficult to see why that privilege should not be extended to ex-players.

It may seem that I am arguing against myself: first I go on endlessly about the tremendous need to keep the amateur line intact, and then I say it should be changed. The difference is that one line concerns the players while the other concerns ex-players. You have to ask: what good is the amateur principle? The short answer is the one I gave at the start of this piece, the 'Monday morning' answer: it protects the players from professionals (or semi-professionals) whose methods and motives were well described by J. J. Williams when he said 'I mean, they don't care, you know?' But that cannot apply to ex-players. For them the application of the amateurism rules is absurdly inconsistent. For instance, the rules make an exception for full-time journalists or broadcasters – but not necessarily *sports* reporters. The agricultural correspondent of the *Daily Telegraph* is exempt; the farmer who reads his column is not. A disc jockey who doubles as a rugby commentator is in the clear; a greengrocer and ex-player who does the same is not. It makes no sense. The exemption that was given to journalists in 1960 should be widened to cover all ex-players.

Other than that, there is no reason to change the amateurism laws. The game has grown and flourished under them for over a century, and whatever strains and tensions may appear at international level, it is worth remembering that this is only a tiny fraction of the hundreds of thousands of games played each year. The laws are for *all* the players, not just the few who are privileged to share the honour and glory of representing their country. Meanwhile, there is one good thing to be said for Rugby League. It offers an escape for all those who are not satisfied with playing the game for its own sake. If they want to play rugby for money, there is always this professional version up the road. Good luck to them. I hope they can still walk on Monday morning.

A blast from the past

There will never be another try like the try that Bob Deans did not score for New Zealand against Wales in 1905.

The scenario was Wagnerian.

It was the first time the two countries had met. Wales held the Triple Crown. So, in a sense, did New Zealand: they had recently beaten Scotland (12-7), Ireland (15-nil) and England (also 15-nil, with five tries). Their tour had opened with a 55-4 walloping of Devon, who were the current English county champions. When the score came down the wire, the Fleet Street news agencies knew it must be a mistake. First editions gave the result as Devon 55, New Zealand 4. This was changed in the second editions, when the All Black victory had been confirmed, to Devon 4, New Zealand 5.

Sports editors soon learned better. The tourists spent a happy three months travelling around the British Isles and leaving all the top clubs in tatters behind them. When they came to play Wales at Cardiff on Saturday, 16 December, the All Blacks had won twenty-seven games in a row. They had piled up 801 points, and only 22 points had been scored against them.

Nothing but Wales stood between the All Blacks and a clean sweep of British rugby. If Wales couldn't beat them it was inconceivable that the last few clubs on the tourists' route would do the trick.

It goes without saying that both teams were stiff with talent, but as it happened the result turned on two strongly contrasting young players. The All Black centre, Bob Deans, was twenty-one. He weighed 13st 4lb and stood six feet tall and the press liked to call him 'the Goliath of the backs'. Teddy Morgan, playing on the wing for Wales, was a medical student. It was said that he was one of the smallest threequarters ever capped by Wales, but it was also said that he was 'the fastest rugby sprinter in the world'.

A third man came in for much scrutiny: the referee. The New Zealand management had rejected all four names put forward by Wales, so Wales applied the International Board's rules and asked Scotland to make the choice. Scotland picked John Dallas. He too was relatively young. He had captained Watsonians, and he had played for Scotland as recently as 1903 – he scored against England – after which he was dropped, not because he was slowing down but because he was considered too fast for a forward at a time when the Scottish policy was to pick beefy scrummagers. Or so the story went. At any rate it's worth noting – in view of what happened later – that nobody, before the match, questioned Dallas's speed or fitness.

The game was, of course, a sell-out. The gates of Cardiff Arms Park were shut on a crowd of 47,000 at 1.30 p.m., an hour before kick-off. The atmosphere crackled with the high voltage of excitement.

The Welsh XV had more to worry about than the All Blacks' brilliant running and handling. There was also the problem of the New Zealand scrum.

The 1905 All Blacks packed down 2-3-2. Both front-row men were hookers. A lock forward bound them together and shoved forward, while the two 'side-row' men shoved inwards. So did the two back-row forwards. The effect was to create a wedge that drove through the orthodox 3-2-3 British scrums like a snowplough.

This wedge pattern was obvious, and several opponents had tried to duplicate it. They failed. 'What they could not see,' said the All Blacks' captain, Dave Gallaher, after the tour, 'and what we would not tell them, was how and where each of these seven – but particularly the side-row and the back-row men – applied their force towards one common centre.' It was, he said, 'a secret which baffled all who played against us, and which every man in the team was sworn to preserve until we had played our last match.'

Quite so. Mind you, the aggressive way the All Black front row battled for the loose head, and won it, made a difference too. It meant that New Zealand always had the advantage at the put-in and the third man in the British front row was useless. Meanwhile the tourists had a spare forward, a rover who could prowl around the scrum as an extra half-back. This occasionally got them into trouble. When they played Surrey the referee was William Williams. (Two years later he bought ten and a quarter acres of market garden in Middlesex on behalf of the RFU. It cost £5572, and some thought it was a great mistake; which is why Twickenham is still known as 'Billy Williams's cabbage patch'.) In the Surrey match Williams took a dim view of the All Blacks' roving forward, Gillett, who (in his opinion) repeatedly obstructed the Surrey half-back. He penalised Gillett twelve times in the first half, which goes some way to explain why the score was only 11-nil.

Nevertheless the All Blacks obviously had a terrific advantage up front. They

A postcard issued to celebrate Wales's 3–nil victory over the All Blacks in 1905. Note that the linesman is in the picture – but where was the referee? The background of empty stands suggests that this photograph was not taken on the day of the match, so Dallas was probably back in Edinburgh.

were disrupting their opponents, winning the ball, heeling it fast – and all with only seven forwards, so they started every attack with an extra man. Dave Gallaher said that after the tour Gwyn Nicholls, the Welsh centre and a great rugby brain, told him Wales had tried to copy the All Blacks' scrum in training: 'They had practised our formation but could get nothing from it.'

When the teams ran on to the field the All Blacks felt the almost physical impact of the roar of a big Celtic crowd. It was like nothing they had ever known. Weeks later, Gallaher recalled the massive, fervent singing of the Welsh national anthem as 'the most impressive incident I have ever witnessed on a football field'. It was a fitting overture to a game that he called 'an Homeric contest of skill, endurance, pace and sheer brute strength – the hardest, keenest struggle I can ever remember'.

From the kick-off, Wales startled the All Blacks by winning a lot of good ball and using it well. The tourists were relieved to see a drop at goal fall just short; then they watched the Welsh right wing, Willie Llewellyn, take a pass with nothing but fresh air between him and the line; but he had to juggle with the ball and it escaped him before he could score.

What's more, all this was done with only seven men in the scrum. Wales had decided to flatter New Zealand by imitation: they took Cliff Pritchard out of the scrum and made him a rover. At the same time they countered the two-man wedge. When the scrums formed, Wales put in five men, packing two and three, and briefly allowed New Zealand to have the loose head: only briefly because a Welsh forward dashed in and made himself the new loose head, with the seventh Welsh forward bound on behind him. Thus Wales packed three and four. New Zealand, deprived of an automatic loose-head advantage, couldn't heel as quickly as usual. Often they couldn't heel at all. After twenty-five minutes they lost a scrum fifteen yards inside their half, and Wales struck.

Until now, Cliff Pritchard – the rover forward – hadn't seen a lot of action; Wales had preferred to spin the ball along the threequarter line. This scrum was quite close to the Welsh right touchline: about fifteen yards from it. Dicky Owen at scrum-half snapped up a quick heel and ran to the blind side with the centre, Gwyn Nicholls, hard behind him and Willie Llewellyn, the winger, poised near touch. The New Zealand defence swung left to plug the gap. Owen checked, turned back, and flung a long pass infield. Cliff Pritchard, going flat out, picked it off his toes and made the first break by swerving past one man. His pass to Gabe was shuttled on to little Teddy Morgan. Morgan sprinted. He beat the All Black cover on the outside, hared down the left wing and scored near the cornerflag.

The explosion of noise was thermonuclear. For the first time in three months and twenty-eight games, the All Blacks were losing.

Wales led by those three points at half-time, and that was still the score when there were only ten minutes left to play. As the second half wore on, the All Blacks won more and more possession, but for once their backs did not match their pack. The threequarters made mistakes; and when they got their act together, the Welsh covering and tackling was endless and relentless.

Then Wales made one small error.

At a line-out just inside the New Zealand half, Wales got possession and someone kicked ahead. W. J. Wallace, the tourists' left wing, caught the ball and raced across the face of the Welsh pack. Wallace had been nicknamed 'Carbine' after a famous New Zealand racehorse, and now he turned on his speed. He cut left, leaving Gwyn Nicholls flatfooted, straightened up and streaked through the defence 'like a mackerel through a shoal of herrings', as one observer remembered.

But not completely. H. B. Winfield, the full-back, was ahead and Willie Llewellyn was closing fast. Wallace committed them both. As Llewellyn slammed into him he passed to Bob Deans, who was storming up on the left.

Deans had thirty yards to go. No Welshman stood between him and a try. All he had to do was run straight.

But Deans wanted to do more than score; he wanted to *win*. If he ran straight he would score midway between the goal and the cornerflag. To make sure of the conversion kick, he swerved towards the posts – and Teddy Morgan.

Morgan was racing in from his wing. If Deans had taken the shortest route Morgan would never have touched him. As it was, Morgan caught him short of the line and brought him down with a thump. Dallas blew his whistle, and it was not for a try.

Half a dozen players were on the scene at once, and in the days and months and years to come, they each produced different versions of what happened. Rhys Gabe, for instance, always believed that *he* had tackled Deans. 'I brought Deans down outside the line,' Gabe claimed, adding that Deans then struggled forward. Gwyn Nicholls agreed; in fact he thought Deans should have been penalised. The situation was confused by the sudden arrival of Welsh reinforcements. A. F. Harding, a forward, added his weight to the tackle, and Percy Bush, a half-back, found the ball and 'replaced it in the exact position in which it had been originally grounded by Deans'. He did this to help the referee, he said, which is enough to make anyone who has ever refereed in Wales extremely suspicious.

However, there was one Welsh player who claimed that Deans really did score, and that was Teddy Morgan himself. The trouble is he didn't say so at the time. It was sixteen years later, in 1921, that he committed himself; and his version of events is unconvincing:

> 'As I tackled him (a few yards outside) I distinctly saw the white goal-line underneath me, and yet, when I got up off Deans's legs, he was holding on to the ball (with two others of our side) which was grounded about a foot outside the line. Dallas, the referee, came running up and had not seen what happened after the tackle.'

It simply doesn't hang together. Morgan could not have tackled Deans 'a few yards outside' *and* seen the line beneath him. It's possible, of course, that Deans was going so hard that his momentum carried them both over the line, but that is not what Morgan says. The implication of his statement is that Deans was brought down over the line and therefore scored, but that 'two others' – Gabe and Harding – dragged him back.

This is the legend of Deans's try that has taken root in New Zealand. It is as much a part of sporting mythology as the 'long count' in the Dempsey–Tunney fight of 1927. Both raised the same cries of 'We wuz robbed!' The difference is that everyone present could see and hear the long count (although few realised that it lasted 14 seconds only because Dempsey took so long retiring to a neutral corner,

England v New Zealand, 1905. An Englishman lunges despairingly while Bob Deans, on the right, gets ready to do his stuff. England lost, but either Deans or the goal-line is in a very odd position.

which was where he had to be before the referee could start counting), whereas nobody in the All Black party felt hard-done-by when Wales won 3-nil on 16 December 1905. And that, surely, is the significant fact: not what was said *afterwards*, but what was *not* said at the time. There is no record of any protest by a New Zealander when Dallas gave a scrum and not a try. Nor did any member of the All Black party comment on the incident at the dinner after the match. It wasn't the players who created the legend of Deans's try. It was the *Daily Mail*.

A brisk circulation-war was going on in Fleet Street in 1905, and one of the weapons of war was the scoop. The big news in the Sunday papers was Wales's victory, but Monday would be another day, another story. The *Daily Mail*'s man in Cardiff – aptly named Buttery – started chatting up anyone he could find, in the hope that some fresh angle might emerge that would give birth to a follow-up sensation which would add a whole new dimension to the result.

Deans found himself talking to Buttery. How close did Deans think he had come to scoring? 'I thought I'd scored,' Deans said. That was enough for Buttery. On Sunday he sent a telegram to the *Daily Mail* in London:

> 'Grounded Ball 6 inches over line some of Welsh players admit try.
> Hunter and Glasgow can confirm was pulled back by Welshmen
> before Referee arrived. Deans.'

Next day the *Mail* had a headline: *Bob Deans says he scored against Wales!*

Hunter and Glasgow were All Black players. They must have reached the scene of Morgan's tackle *after* Gabe, Harding and Bush got there, for there is no mention anywhere of a New Zealander other than Deans being involved in the incident, so they were not ideally placed to see what had happened. Indeed, only one man *was* ideally placed, and he was the referee.

We can ignore Morgan's confident assertion that Dallas 'had not seen what had happened after the tackle'. How did Morgan knows what Dallas saw? Morgan's attention was all on Deans, and after the tackle Morgan's face was probably either jammed against Deans's legs or pressed in the mud.

We can also forget all the snide remarks made by later generations about the referee's dress. Dallas wore what every referee wore in 1905: sensible street clothes and stout boots. He was fit and he had no difficulty keeping up with play; indeed the press reports acknowledged his competence in keeping a good grip on what was a fast and furious game.

When Wallace made his break, Dallas ran with him. He was on Wallace's right when Deans caught the final pass. Dallas then took the most direct path to the line. Obviously a try was on, and the best place for a referee when that happens is over

Dave Gallaher, captain of the 1905 All Blacks.
His book of the tour made no complaints – and
not a word about Deans.

the goal-line. 'When the ball went back on its way to Deans I kept going hard,' Dallas wrote afterwards, 'and when Deans was tackled he grounded the ball six to twelve inches short of the goal-line.'

Dallas blew his whistle. He did not – as Morgan and Deans believed – run over to the mêlée and *then* make his decision, based on what he saw when he got there. He saw Deans brought down short and so he immediately blew up to order a scrum. Why a scrum was the appropriate thing to have in those circumstances is another matter. The important point is that Dallas, from a distance, saw that Deans had not scored and he blew up. What happened after that is irrelevant, because the ball was dead. Dallas had no doubts about his decision, and it seems certain that it was not questioned after the match, because he wrote later: 'On

Monday morning I was astonished to read in the papers on my return to Edinburgh, that Deans had "scored" a try that I had disallowed.'

After the tour, Dave Gallaher and his vice-captain, W. J. Stead, wrote a book. Reading between the lines, one gets the impression that they wished the Deans story would go away. About the Welsh match they said: 'It is not our place now to make excuses for this defeat . . . ' In their opinion the team had been stale, and the players had become affected by the burden of their unbeaten record. 'When we made an ineffectual start, and the Welshmen from the beginning showed a wonderful amount of dash and fire, something very much like nervousness crept into our side . . . Pass after pass went wrong. The forwards, indeed, were sound enough . . . but . . . the backs were hopelessly off colour . . . '

Not a word about Deans.

New Zealand completed the tour by winning the last four games, although each was a tremendous struggle: they beat Glamorgan 9-nil, Newport 6-3, Cardiff 10-8 and Swansea 4-3. They had played thirty-two games and conceded only seven tries. The try that really hurt was, of course, Teddy Morgan's.

I don't suppose the myth of Deans's alleged try will ever die. It's been told and re-told too often. New Zealanders who visit Cardiff Arms Park often make a pilgrimage to the actual spot where it happened and gaze at those few square feet of sacred turf. Here the eternal drama of attack and defence reached its greatest climax. Here Deans and Morgan completed their mighty collision-course. Here was the site of the supreme test of the 1905 tour.

Except that it wasn't. Cardiff Arms Park has been restructured since 1905, and the spot where Morgan stopped Deans is no longer in the field of play. Nobody seems very sure where exactly it is, but the best guess is somewhere underneath the men's lavatories. Or is that another myth?

Cocking up a good game

It's remarkable how such mature, sane, intelligent men as rugby players can take what is a fundamentally simple and enjoyable game and, by sheer determination and ingenuity, succeed in cocking it up.

History is littered with these examples of attempted suicide.

I'll pass over such self-inflicted wounds as ignoring the development of the four-threequarter system in the hope that it would give up and go away. No, I shan't: it's too fascinating, in a gruesome way. Cardiff picked young F. E. Hancock in 1884 when one of their regular *three* threequarters got hurt. Hancock scored twice. After that, Cardiff wanted to keep him but they didn't want to drop the regular man, now recovered; so they used them all and played Hancock as a *fourth* threequarter. The system worked. Next season Cardiff won 26 matches out of 27, scored 131 tries, conceded 4. Other Welsh clubs copied Cardiff, but in England the new system was known as 'the Welsh Abortion', even after Wales – with four threequarters – beat England for the first time, in 1890.

But that was simply a matter of tactical blindness. Far worse was the almost universal attempt to bore the game to death with unlimited touch-kicking.

It has a long history. In 1919, New Zealand and New South Wales urged the International Board to change the laws. 'Kicking into touch on the least excuse by a leading side has tended to make a farce of the game in many instances,' they said. 'The use of the touch-line has not shown skill in actual practice, but has rather tended to eliminate skill and keep the ball out of play more than in play.' (Old Rugby League joke: *Question* – 'Where's the best place to catch the ball in Rugby Union?' *Answer* – 'In the stand.') The proposal from Down Under – that direct touch-kicking outside the kicker's 25 should bring no gain in ground – was thrown out.

This didn't mean that the rest of the world was not putting its boot to the ball far too often. When Wavell Wakefield wrote *Rugger* in 1930 it was only a couple of years since he had won the last of his thirty-one caps, and he agreed with the basis of the New Zealand complaint: there was 'excessive kicking into touch'. But he favoured a totally different solution. Excessive touch-kicking is bad, he said, because 'by putting the ball into touch, possession is given to the other side'. The way to stop this, Wakefield argued, is to make such possession more valuable to the non-kicking side; and he proposed that instead of having a line-out 'they should be allowed to re-start play by a punt or a drop-kick in any direction, or a pass straight out or back'. For instance, the player responsible for re-starting the game 'might decide to cross-kick or pass back, or do anything, in short, which seemed the best way of striking at the defence . . . in this way the general knowledge of the game would be increased, a team would be kept on the alert, and individual judgment and skill would be improved.'

Wakefield's thinking was ingenious, and it would be interesting to see the idea tried out. But the IB had no time for ingenuity or experiment. New Zealand and New South Wales had tried to change the touch-kicking law again in 1926 and failed. Ten years later they got permission to adopt the change in their own domestic rugby (they'd been playing it for years anyway). The Home Unions called it 'the Australian Dispensation' or 'the Antipodean Dispensation': shades of the Welsh Abortion.

The offside laws didn't help. Until the 1960s the backs were allowed to lie up flat on a line through the tunnel of the scrum or through the line of the line-out. Back-row forwards could break and follow the ball as their opponents heeled it. Half-backs had precious little time or room to move in, so it's not surprising that they made the most of possession by hoofing the ball into touch.

The logical result of all this was the England–South Africa match of 1961. A jumbo Springbok pack manufactured ball which their half-backs monotonously kicked into touch. There was one score, a bulldozing try from short range by a forward.

In 1962 the Calcutta Cup match lured more than eighty thousand people to Murrayfield. The Triple Crown was at stake. Both sides lay up so flat in defence that all enterprise was stifled, each side kicked a penalty goal, and it's hard to believe the teams weren't as bored as the crowd.

The supreme example of players' staunch and selfless determination to cock up a good game, no matter how much it hurts, came in 1963. Clive Rowlands captained Wales at scrum-half when they went to Murrayfield. Rowlands could kick. He was known in the valleys as 'Clive the Kick', and elsewhere as 'Dai Ding-Dong'. When the international match was over many people went away calling him several other names too.

The Welsh backs might as well have brought their knitting for all the action they saw that afternoon. The Welsh pack gave Rowlands the ball and Rowlands put it into touch. There were one hundred and eleven line-outs. The ball moved in a hemstitch pattern: line-out to Rowlands to touch, line-out to Rowlands to touch, over and over again. Wales won 6-nil without scoring a try. Rugby lost, heavily. Six years later – and fifty years after it was first proposed – the Home Unions adopted the Australian Dispensation.

The scrummage has always been a good place to start cocking up the game. I describe elsewhere the dottiness of fighting for the loose head, and 'Run Round'; and I've already mentioned the license to kill awarded to the back row. This latter was having its tedious effect as long ago as the Edwardian era, when top clubs began breeding forwards who could run like threequarters and thus hound the life out of the enemy backs. Scores were low. Even when leading English sides, like Blackheath or the Harlequins, met their Welsh counterparts, like Newport or Cardiff, it was rare to see more than half a dozen points on the board. There were plenty of nil-nil draws. (So much for the golden age of rugby.) The pattern persisted between the wars. One reason Rugby League kept trying to invade Wales was the dullness (and dirtiness) of much Rugby Union football. You were as likely to see a sending-off as a good try. Eventually the grey futility of it all even reached the players. In the late thirties a few Welsh clubs made gentlemen's agreements to give their backs a better chance to run with the ball: the flank forwards would remain bound to the scrum until the ball was heeled and clear.

But for true lunacy you couldn't beat the put-in to the front rows of the scrum.

Inside every chunky, dour, taciturn front-row forward there is a raving eccentric trying to get out. And inside every neat and well-spoken scrum-half there is a bomb-throwing anarchist plotting the destruction of civilisation as we know it. Together they have been responsible for the breakdown of more referees than sex and age combined.

In the 1890s Swansea had the two James brothers at half-back. 'I admired very much their adroitness at putting the ball into the scrummage,' wrote a reporter after Swansea had taken Llanelli apart. 'They always take care to swing it in . . . well under the back rank of their forwards.'

Nobody expects a scrum-half to be fair, decent, accurate and honest – I mean, you wouldn't want your daughter to marry one – but the James brothers were pushing their luck. A few years later, when Dickie Owen was working the scrum for Wales, he got penalised so often for crooked feeds that he gave up and let the opposing scrum-half have the ball at all the scrums.

By the 1920s front-row play had become highly sophisticated; so sophisticated, in fact, that it was often impossible to get the ball in at all. The International Board

debated the problem endlessly. Some said it was all the fault of near-foot hooking. Some said the scrum-half stood too far away. Some said he threw the ball too hard. Others claimed that swinging both legs was the root of the trouble.

There was much drawing of diagrams and labelling of legs – ABCD for one prop and hooker, WXYZ for their opponents. In 1931 the IB came to the conclusion that everything would be satisfactory if only the referee would apply the law. Since the England–Scotland match was coming up soon, the IB sent a sub-committee to meet the referee and the two captains and explain the damn thing to them in words of one syllable.

This they did, and it made matters worse. The game was a fiasco. The ball refused to go into the scrum and everyone was thoroughly confused, above all the England captain and hooker, Sam Tucker, who said afterwards that he had never been so scared in his life. 'During the whole game,' he said, 'I never knew what I could do or couldn't do.'

'In 1931,' wrote Admiral Sir Percy Royds in his history of the laws, 'the number of attempts that had to be made before the ball got properly into the scrummage was remarked on after every match that was played.'

The problem – like all good problems – had three parts: hooking, trapping and feeding.

The law said that the hooker must not strike until the ball was fairly in the scrum. To reach that happy state it had to go in straight, touch the ground and pass both feet of one player of each team. So much for hooking.

Trapping was a lot tougher. The law said that the first three feet of the front-row forwards of each team must not be raised or moved forward until the ball had passed them. Three-legged props being thin on the ground, this meant that hookers were not supposed to use the nearer foot until the ball had reached the farther foot.

And that was not a speedy journey – not if the scrum-half did what the law told him to do. It laid down that he should *gently propel* the ball into the tunnel.

That, of course, was where the whole performance blew a fuse. As soon as the ball started trickling into the tunnel, the front-row forwards enjoyed a rush of blood to the head and forgot the small print that the lawmakers at the IB had so patiently composed. The front rows saw the ball, and they struck. They were, after all, only human. Well, sub-human.

Through that welter of striking legs the ball could not go. It usually ricocheted out or got kicked out, not once but several times.

The seasons came and went, and there was little improvement. Eminent men agonised over the problem of getting the ball into the scrum. To give you something of the flavour of their deliberations, here is clause (k)(3) of a new scrummage law proposed by the RFU in 1932:

> The NEARER FOOT of the MIDDLE PLAYER of each front row and EITHER FOOT of the player NEAREST the side on which the ball is put in must not be raised or advanced to obtain possession until the ball has touched the FARTHER FOOT of the MIDDLE front row player or a foot of a player beyond.

It reads like part of a correspondence course in how to do the tango.

The RFU's proposals were not accepted, but the way that the clause was worded goes a long way towards explaining the general lack of progress. The lawmakers didn't speak the same language as the players. They talked about *the middle player* and *the player beyond* rather than the hooker and the prop because they didn't approve of having hookers and props. In 1932 the IB, having decided not to change the scrummage law, sent a circular to players, referees and the press. It said:

'The Board are of opinion that the difficulties arising, especially in and about the scrummage, are largely, if not entirely, due to the practice of over-specialisation by forwards, such as securing a fixed formation in the scrummage . . . '

The Board also gave scrum-halves stick for putting the ball in 'with unnecessary force' when gently propelling it, they stressed, was quite adequate. But it was this modern craze for 'over-specialization' that really got up the IB's nose. They damned it as the cause of 'a serious deterioration in forward play'. The scrummage suffered, they said, when a forward accustomed to playing in one position didn't appreciate the duties of those playing in other positions. The Board strongly urged an end to this practice, and went on:

'It is convinced that the old principle of "first up, first down" should be revived in order not only to cultivate the qualities of grit and determination, but also to discover the most promising material, and to impress on that material the importance of genuine scrummaging . . . '

The appeal failed. If anything, it became even harder to get the ball into the scrum. The veterans on the IB wanted to bring back the good old days of innocence when scrums were a matter of simple, honest shoving; but nostalgia was no answer to the problems created by change.

The whole thing was a mess. In 1935, Royds notes, there was still 'great difficulty in getting the ball into the scrummage and an entire misunderstanding of the law, and total disinclination to observe it'. In 1937 the RFU reported to the IB that there was 'great variance in the interpretation of Law 15 [the scrummage law], and this is having a serious affect [sic] on the game all over the country'. Meetings, experiments, proposals continued. The RFU made a film of the ball going into a scrum, in order to prove a point it felt was important, and sent copies to the other Home Unions. Ireland replied that a film didn't prove anything, Wales replied that they didn't see any reason for viewing the film, and Scotland didn't reply.

Came 1939, and the IB took another stab at the problem. All the member Unions had their say, and the Irish had four says because Leinster, Connaught, Munster and Ulster each thought differently. There were many opinions about the scrum-half's speed of feed: some wanted 'moderate', some wanted 'slow', and some said it didn't matter a damn because the scrum-half would pitch the ball into the tunnel at his own sweet speed whatever the law said, just as he had always done. At that point the meeting was adjourned for the Second World War. This seems to have concentrated minds wonderfully. When normal service resumed in 1946 the Unions managed to sort out the scrum problem relatively quickly. So ended an amazingly long chapter of nonsense.

But if players couldn't cock up the scrum, there was still the lineout.

In the 1960s the lineout law was changed to allow the team throwing in to decide its length. If they opted for a full line-out, using all eight forwards, their opponents could also put in eight (or, if they wished, fewer). If they opted for a short line-out, using only two men, their opponents had to match this. The key figure was the furthest player in the line-out of the team throwing in. He was the 'backmarker'. Any opposing lineout player who stood behind him was offside.

There were good reasons for this change, and it worked pretty well for about five minutes.

Then the Einsteins of coarse rugby made a wonderful discovery. Given a line-out a yard from their own goal-line, they put in all their forwards. Naturally, the other team matched them. One second before the ball was thrown in, six of the eight defending forwards sprang back across their goal-line, leaving their opponents inevitably off-side. Penalty kick.

The stupidity of it was obvious. One team was being penalised, not for doing anything wrong, but because the other team had twisted the law. It was a cheap little trick, and it soiled the game for a year until it was stopped. But one reason why that sort of childish sabotage was possible was the IB's notorious reluctance either to test law changes in advance or to explain and justify them when they were introduced. I remember many a fascinating evening at my local rugby referees' society as we held the latest changes up to the light and wondered what the hell the IB was trying to achieve. The Board told us *what* but they didn't say *why*. It was as

if – like doctors, lawyers and tax accountants – they jealously guarded the secrets of their calling. If they had shared the mystery with us, the common footsoldiers of the game, then there would have been no mystery, and they would have suffered a dreadful blow to their prestige. That wasn't on. And so, every year, the revised tablets were handed down from the mountainside.

Unfortunately the Board was not God, or even Moses. Sometimes they stumbled.

Readers of a nervous disposition should skip the next bit, otherwise they're liable to end up lying in a darkened room with damp towels on their heads, while servants spread straw in the street to muffle the horse-traffic and loved ones search the bathroom cabinet for the extra-strength pain-relievers.

It happened in 1976. The IB wanted to change the lineout law, in particular the law covering a ruck or maul that formed in a lineout. When the new lawbooks came out, referees and players discovered that a ruck or maul forming in a lineout was *not* now a ruck or maul but a continuation on the lineout. Even if the ruck/maul moved away from the original place of the lineout, the new law said that the line-out had not legally ended (despite the fact that it had vanished).

The question that sprang to the minds of players and referees was: What about off-side? At a lineout, the offside line for the threequarters was ten yards back. If the line-out hadn't ended, that offside line still applied, since there had been no change to the original lineout laws.

It was easy to imagine how a line-out could lead to a maul and the maul could move ten yards upfield – but the attacking team's back line must now stay ten yards behind the original lineout position until the ball emerged from the maul! Thus the team that won possession *and* territory would be penalised by being prevented from bringing its threequarters into the attack.

Nor was that all. For the players taking part in the line-out there was confusion over exactly when and where *they* might be off-side. The IB said that for a ruck/maul-in-a-lineout (which wasn't technically a ruck/maul but wasn't visibly a lineout) the offside line ran through the ball. However, the existing law said that a line-out ended when the ball travelled more than fifteen yards infield from the touch-line. Suppose a ruck/maul-in-a-lineout lurched sideways until it crossed that fifteen-yard line. Clearly the lineout was over. So what was left? It must be an old-fashioned ruck or maul. And where did the offside line run in that case? Not through the ball. It ran through the hindmost foot.

So in the space of a quick lurch, a forward could go from being on-side (behind the ball) to being off-side (in front of the hindmost foot).

There were several other confusions, which I'll spare you. The upshot of the whole shambles was the IB scrapped the change. What they could not do was take it out of print. 'I hope players have not torn up last season's handbooks yet,' said Dudley Kemp, one of England's men on the Board.

I don't want to give the impression that rugby is full of noble souls, all trying desperately hard to play up and play the game, despite the interference of the IB. All too often it works the other way around: the Board does its best and the players do their worst. Take, for instance, the manner in which Newport beat the All Blacks 3-nil in 1963. *Rugby Under Pressure,* by Brian Jones and Ian McJennett, summarised the Newport match-plan:

> '. . . any loose ball on the floor would be killed. This is where Glyn Davidge won his glory and his bruises. Before the All Blacks could be driving over the ball, they had to get him out of the way. We calculated that under British interpretations as they then existed,

New Zealand would be more likely to concede a penalty for kicking the man on the floor than Davidge would be for holding on too long. When the whistle went for a set-scrum, we were more likely to be given the put-in as the defending side. In the match, this was to be what happened.'

The result was treated in Wales as a great victory. As Chris Laidlaw, the All Black scrum-half in a later tour, pointed out, Newport's tactics were the negation of rugby. (He made the same comment of the Llanelli–New Zealand match in 1972.) If players were allowed to stifle rucks by lying on or over the ball, there could be no second-phase play. Little wonder that the All Black packs stopped discriminating between man and ball in the rucks and simply rucked out both in one writhing, moaning package.

All the self-inflicted wounds that I've described so far have been understandable if not forgivable, because they all took place within the framework of the laws. There remains the matter of winning by going outside the laws. By cheating.

The way New Zealand beat Wales in 1978 – Haden's melodramatic dive from a line-out in the closing minutes, when Wales were leading 12-10, and the penalty goal that gave New Zealand the match 12-13 – was a sign of a new and different approach to cocking up a great game. Graham Mourie captained the All Blacks that day. In his autobiography he relates the background to Haden's dive. Mourie is remarkably frank. He makes no bones about it: the night before the international, he and Haden talked about the trick of winning undeserved penalties by diving from line-outs.

What Mourie specifically referred to was a match in 1966 between Taranaki and King Country. In the first half, Colin Meads gave the Taranaki forwards a lot of trouble in the line-outs. At half time J. J. Stewart, the Taranaki (and later All Black) coach, suggested a way of winning penalties: throw the ball to Meads, and as he caught it let Eliason, a Taranaki forward, stagger loudly out of the line-out. Eliason performed his act and Taranaki kicked three penalties to win 20-12.

It seems that the ploy was something of a joke – it was the last game of the season – and there was much suppressed laughter. (Not from Meads. Afterwards, he was extremely angry. He told Eliason: 'That's the dirtiest trick I've ever seen on a rugby field!') It was no joke at Cardiff Arms Park in 1978.

Mourie concedes that his pack was outplayed on the day, and that Wales had seventy per cent of the ball. Nevertheless New Zealand recovered from 12-7 at half time to 12-10 with time running out. 'I knew we could win,' he wrote, 'but how to get the points? How were we to score?'

The night before, after he and Haden had discussed Eliason's trick, Mourie had told him: 'We might need something like that sometime.' Now New Zealand won a line-out on the Welsh 22. Haden spoke to his team-mate Oliver.

The ball was thrown in and three things happened at the same time. Oliver went down. Haden dived outwards. The referee gave New Zealand a penalty.

In the pandemonium of the moment, most people thought Roger Quittenton had penalised someone for barging Haden. Barry John, who was taking part in the television commentary, was furious at what he called 'the biggest con of all time' — he had seen Haden dive. In fact Quittenton had penalised Geoff Wheel for leaning on Oliver's shoulder. Haden's dive had nothing to do with the penalty.

McKechnie kicked the goal and to that extent New Zealand deserved to win. All the same it was a shabby, seedy way to make sure of winning. The fact that Roger Quittenton got it right does not excuse the All Blacks for getting it wrong. If Haden had tricked a penalty out of the referee as Eliason had done, the All Blacks would have claimed victory just the same. And yet it cannot be victory when one side deliberately cheats in order to score. They may end up with more points, but what have they won? Certainly not a game of rugby. They haven't been playing rugby. No doubt some skill is involved in faking a foul, but it's not a rugby skill. 'When you are on tour,' Mourie concluded, 'it is of little importance discussing moral questions.' He deceives himself. He was discussing a moral question with Haden on the night before the match. He was discussing how to cheat.

Socked in

The best match I never saw was England Schoolboys v Australian Schoolboys. The three Ella brothers were in the tourists' team, and their interplay was so brilliant that they were rumoured to be telepathic. They needed to be, that day. They certainly couldn't see each other. Twickenham was fogged in. Even the seagulls were grounded. The match took place only because the stadium was stuffed full of restless schoolboys who had travelled from all over England; they had to be given *some*thing. They got the odd glimpse of a vague figure vanishing into the murk, plus periodic announcements of Australian scores. It wasn't enough. The lads sitting behind me grew bored with fog and defeat and began pelting each other with their sandwiches. For me, the most exciting moment of the afternoon was when half a round of cheese-and-chutney hit me in the ear.

That day aside, Twickenham has been amazingly lucky with the elements. I may be wrong, but as far as I can discover the weather has never stopped an international match being played there. This is the more remarkable because the ground at Twickenham is low-lying, and until its banks were built up the local river – the Crane – had a habit of flooding the land. 1927 was a wet winter, and at times the Crane was flowing through the west car park to a depth of several feet.

Later that year the weather turned bitterly cold, and only a thick layer of straw on the pitch saved the match with Ireland. But conditions at Twickenham – that 'remote and inaccessible theatre of warfare' *The Times* had called it in 1912 – have been good more often than not. If days of rain turned the surface into a bog (as happened to the Wales game in 1939) the worst that critics could say was that Twickenham was almost as bad as Cardiff Arms Park. But even Welshmen had to include that 'almost'. When the rainstorms came hulking up the Bristol Channel there was no quagmire like the Arms Park. The sound of thirty men and the referee pulling their boots out of the mud was like porridge boiling over. When England went to Cardiff in 1922 there were more pools than grass, and the pools were so deep that the referee blew up the rucks fast, before someone drowned.

Frost and fog were the real threats at Twickenham. It was touch-and-go in 1947: the winter had been arctic, and the pitch was still frozen when Scotland came down in mid-March. Nobody was match-fit. There were injuries galore – at one point both teams were down to thirteen men. Conditions were, if anything, worse in March 1952 for the match against Ireland. The ground was like iron and a blizzard was blowing. In a normal year the game would have been postponed, but this particular fixture had been postponed once already, because of the death of George VI, so it went ahead.

There was a bit of fog about when England played New Zealand in 1964 but not enough to obscure anything memorable – it was a dull match – and this only served to emphasise how lucky Twickenham has been. The peasoupers that used to get brewed up by the smoke of a million open fires seemed always to avoid international days. Not so the University match. Before they moved the fixture to Twickenham, Oxford and Cambridge played at the Queen's Club ground in London, usually in fog. Their 1919 game began in a mist and ended in a murk that was so dense the players found each other by shouting. (Even that was capped by the Otley v Headingley game of December 1934, when the fog came down like Hammer Films on overtime. After the match they held a roll-call in the dressing-rooms. Two players didn't answer. A search-party went out and found them still standing on the pitch, waiting for the ball. Or so they say.)

But nothing compared with the great blot-out of 1908.

Twickenham hadn't been invented then. The RFU played its home internationals on the grounds of the leading clubs: Blackheath, Manchester, Leeds, Dewsbury, Birkenhead, Gloucester, and the like. Bristol wanted a place in the sun.

Bristol had no big rugby ground, but Bristol City FC was willing to let the RFU use its soccer stadium. The England–Wales game was scheduled to be played at Bristol on 18 January 1908. In one respect it looked like a good idea: the gate-money was a record, and the crowd was reckoned at between twenty and thirty thousand. But the estimate was vague because nobody could actually see all the crowd. Nobody could see both sets of goal posts. When the teams ran out nobody could see all the players. That was at the start, when the fog wasn't too bad. Later, there were long spells when many spectators couldn't see *any* of the players.

The Bristol City ground lies in a bowl. As usual, the surrounding citizens had stoked up their fires with plenty of coal against the winter chill, and the hills trapped the sulphurous fumes. There was no breeze. Long before the kick-off people were telling each other the game would never be played. When Percy Bush, the Welsh outside-half, arrived and a journalist asked him which way Wales would be playing, he said: 'We will play with the fog.'

It turned out to be an accurate prediction. Wales won 28–18, scoring five tries (two converted), a dropped goal and a penalty; but one reporter wrote that he saw none of the Welsh scores. 'Never was it possible to see all the players of either side; there was not one combined movement of which we saw both the beginning and the end. A thickening and thinning of the fog made visibility variable; but at the best it was barely possible to see halfway across the field, at the worst figures moving through the fog ten yards from the touch-line were but dimly seen.' From time to time the touch-judge gave pressmen news of scores and scorers. Cross-kicks soared into the gloom and vanished; kicks at goal came out of nowhere, kicked by invisible men; passes were swallowed by the fog. Brilliance or blunder, missed tackle or interception, jinking run or clumsy fumble – few people saw them, and fewer still could identify the players. This was the most secret international of them all.

Percy Bush soon worked out how to 'play with the fog'. At one point he threw a long pass to Rhys Gabe, his centre, and while Gabe headed left into obscurity, Bush ran right, uttering urgent Celtic cries as he went. While the English backs homed-in on the noise, Gabe scored between the posts.

All told, nine tries were scored that afternoon – more than in any England–Wales match since their first, absurdly lopsided meeting in 1881. As one Welshman shrewdly said: 'It must have been a great game.' For an afternoon largely spent staring at yellow fog, it seems to have made a powerful impression on those present. One such was the sportswriter W. J. T. Collins, better known to his readers in South Wales as 'Dromio'. In 1948 the match was still fresh – if not clear – in his memory:

> 'Even to-day, to think of this match brings a sort of chill in the blood and mist in the mind. On land or sea, whether alone on a mountain or one of an anxious crowd on a steamer, fog inspires an eerie feeling; and as I think of the foggy international of forty years ago I am reminded of "The Passing of Arthur" and that other "dim, weird battle of the West" when "friend and foe were shadows in the mist".'

One thing was not shadowy: the result. Swanning around the country from club to club was not the way to build a team. Two years later England invited Wales to Twickenham. England won 11-6, and went on beating Wales at home for the next twenty-three years. No fog at Twickers; at least, not on match-days. There may be some dispute over whether God is an Englishman, but by God there's no doubt that he's a rugby supporter.

Shame on him

The Argentine national team are not the Pumas. They are the Jaguars. The animal shown on their jerseys is a jaguar, but when they toured South Africa in 1966 some dim journalist got it wrong and now the name has stuck.

Another myth is that Mick English, the Ireland fly-half of the late fifties, once caught a hyphen. The story is that Ireland were playing England, and Mick went to tackle his opposite number, John Horrocks-Taylor, but 'the Horrocks went one way and the Taylor went the other, and I was left holding the hyphen!' Alas, the two men never faced each other in an international; indeed, Horrocks-Taylor was never selected against Ireland. But there are not all that many clean rugby jokes, so this one will probably endure.

So too will the myth of the haka. It is not a traditional Maori war dance. It is more like a calypso. But it looks like a war dance, it sounds like a war dance, and by God every spectator wants it to be a war dance, so fat chance that anyone will ever permit himself to be confused with the facts.

Here, nevertheless, are the facts.

There is not one haka. (Incidentally, the word describes the total performance: both dance and lyrics.) There are many different hakas. Certainly the Maoris used to let rip with a good lusty haka as they prepared to do battle, but they also performed other hakas to welcome visitors, say, or to entertain people. Like the calypso it's a very flexible form. The East Coast Maoris applied it to political ends when they composed an anti-prohibition haka in the early twenties. (It was called 'the Haka Poropiehana', if you want to order the music.)

What, then, of that sinister-looking, fist-clenching, knee-pounding, grunt-and-shout haka that the All Blacks deliver before kick-off, while their opponents nervously buff their fingernails and wonder why they hadn't taken up a more sensible sport, such as the clarinet? The meaning is perfectly straight-forward:

93

Ka mate ka mate ka ora ka ora
Ka mate ka mate ka ora ka ora
Te nei te ta nga ta pu huru huru
Na na e piki mai whaka white te ra
Hu pa nei, hu ka nei, hu pa nei kau
pa nei white te ra!

You can't say fairer than that, can you? Well, it seems that you can. Not everyone is agreed on the finer philosophical points that you find so blindingly obvious. The RFU newspaper *Rugby Post*, for instance, offers this translation:

'tis death, 'tis death
'tis life, 'tis life. (*repeat*)
This is the man, the hairy man
Coming into the light of the sun.
One step forward.
Onward. (*repeat*)
At last the night.

Haka, 1888 version. Next time they got a proper choreographer.

That's not bad. All Black rugby is not, of course, a matter of life and death – it's far more important than that – but the rest of the words have a nice blend of Cro-Magnon benevolence and juggernaut resolve. The trouble is the last line. When they finish the haka the All Blacks leap in the air with a great shout. Is that leap compatible with the downbeat ethos of *At last the night*? No, no. Somebody got his thumb caught in the word processor. It won't do.

If your literary taste runs to images of scenic grandeur, you might like the translation that Major Leonard Tosswill (three caps for England in 1902) recorded when the All Blacks toured Britain in 1925:

> The New Zealand storm is about to break;
> We shall stand as children of the sun;
> We shall fly to the heavens in exultation;
> We shall attain the zenith!
> The power, the power, the power!

To my ear, that sounds oddly like the kind of heroic revolutionary verse that used to reach the Top 20 in Communist countries. Full of uplift and mixed metaphors.

The test is to ask yourself if you can picture a line of All Blacks urging each other to fly to the heavens in exultation. I've tried, and it isn't easy.

A version of the 1905 All Blacks' haka seems more promising –

> It is death! It is death!
> It is life! It is life!
> This is the strong one!
> He has caused the sun to shine!

– but what it gains in virtue it lacks in subtlety. A haka should give you something to think about, and then make you think twice. That is why I recommend the translation provided by Dave Gallaher, skipper of the 1905 tourists:

> Together we live, together we die.
> This man we bring is the murderous one,
> He slew as long as the sun shone.
> So shame on him! Shame on him!
> Shame on him as long as the sun shines!

Do they really mean what they say? Or is it a coded signal to the opposition? It reminds me of standing in the gents before a match, alongside a large and hairy opponent, who carefully shook the drops off the end and confided in a hoarse whisper: 'You want to watch out for our tight-head prop. He shouldn't be playing, not after what he did last week. Bloody disgrace to the game, if you ask me.' Which I hadn't, of course; but I got the message just the same.

Play up, you Old Sods!

My local club is Chipping Sodbury RFC. Very sensibly, they call themselves the Old Sods. If they didn't, others would; and so in a sense they get their retaliation in first.

Not that Old Sods is, by the standards of rugby football, a peculiar name; not when you look at the Old Haberdashers, the Old Pomfretians, the Old Culverhazians, or the Old Shootershillians. And if you can get your tongue around the Old Mid-Whitgiftians, the Old Westbridgfordians, and the Old Henliensians, try turning it loose on the Old Hurst-Johnians, the Old Oadby-Wyggestonians, and the Old Plymouthians and Mannameadians.

But even these appear ordinary in comparison with some of the really imaginative (that is, unsuitable) names that clubs have chosen. The twenty clubs that formed the RFU in 1871 included Hornets, Gipsies, Mohicans and Flamingoes, all now extinct. I thought the Flamingoes had made the least dynamic choice of an animal until I heard of the Dodo RFC in Mauritius.

There used to be some very odd titles indeed. In 1884 the London German Gymnastic RFC existed (and was good enough to play Cardiff). The junior Welsh clubs of those days were like modern rock groups in their search for original names: Nil Desperandum RFC in Swansea, New Dock Strollers in Llanelli, Troedyrhin Searchlights in Merthyr, and Cwmbran Black Watch in Pontypool (presumably full of Scots immigrants). There were some unlikely combinations too, such as Pontnewynydd Lilies of the Valley, and Panteg Artillery. And occasionally the inventors went over the top, so that Rhymney had the Salmon Tin Dribblers and the Pig's Bladder Barbarians while Carmarthen got the Diamond Skull Crackers. Cornwall – another Celtic stronghold – had a club that could have existed nowhere else: it was called Up-a-long, Down-a-long RFC. Come to think of it, the rest of the chorus to 'Widdicombe Fair' sounds a bit like a Cornish team secretary checking off his 3rd XV late on a Friday night: *Bill Brewer, Jan Stewer, Peter Gurney, Peter Davey, Dan'l Whidden, Harry Hawke . . . Hang on, that's*

only six. Who've I missed? Oh yes . . . Old Uncle Tom Cobbleigh and all . . . In other words: he'll find the rest in the morning.

Of course the Welsh have an unfair advantage. While the rest of the world adds vowels to names to make them speakable, the Welsh pack theirs with consonants to make them unspeakable by anyone who hasn't got a leek stuffed up his trouserleg. Hence Ystralifera. And Llwynypia, a club that produced a good few Welsh caps in the early years. And the more accessible Nantyglo, which I long believed to be a kind of smokeless fuel. On the other hand there is the marvellously apt Pill Harriers. 'Pill' really means a creek, and the original harriers were cross-country runners, but it's still a better name than most committees could dream up in a year.

In the more far-flung corners of the rugby world the clubs have names that look like anagrams in an Albanian crossword. (Albania seems to be one of the few countries where they don't play rugby; on the other hand Albanians are so secretive that anything is possible.) Jugoslavia has a club called Crvena Zvezda, which probably sounds better after a shot of slivovitz; and Tonga has one called Houmakelika. East Germany has its Dynamo Potsdam (boring) and Kenya has its Nondescripts (so boring that it's almost interesting) while Israel can offer Kibbutz Yizreel RFC, probably the only side that grows its own half-time oranges.

Inevitably, national characteristics show through. Who else but Switzerland would have a club called Heidelberg Magicians? Where else but Sweden would you find one named after Attila? (The Swedes, like all well-organised, affluent,

law-abiding people are secretly furious with everyone and would love to have an enormous fight; but they know it's not on.)

There's a club in Pennsylvania called the Bethlehem Hooligans; and another that's listed, with disarming simplicity, as Berks RFC. North Carolina has a women's rugby club called the Charlotte Harlots (motto: *We play the field*) and Virginia has its Turkey Thicket RFC, which is almost, but not quite, as quaint as the First Troop Philadelphia City Cavalry RFC. Moving upmarket, there's a Los Angeles Executives RFC and a Chicago Oxfords RFC. I once refereed a California club called the Foothill Coyotes. They played just the way they sounded.

Bombay has a club called Armenians, which is about as foreign as you can get, and Hong Kong boasts the Flying Kukris RFC, which doesn't sound nearly as inscrutable as one might expect. On the other hand it's reassuring to discover the existence of the Barbados Night Club RFC. I mean, that's what it's all about, innit?

I suppose there is something special to be said for the men who keep the game alive in the town of its birth – Rugby Rugby Football Club – but I can't think of it, so I'll move on to the Irish. Two names deserve special mention. One is Garryowen, the only club to have a tactic named after it; and the other is the delightful Sunday's Well, which sounds like a sigh of gratitude from a prop who's woken up to discover that he survived not only the game but also the party afterwards. Not forgetting also the town of Donnybrook, which if it hasn't got a rugby club, damn well ought to.

Robinson's law of thermodynamic rugby

Robinson's Law of Thermodynamic Rugby states that *every time you bring in a new law of the game it takes seven years for the old law to die out.* Or longer.

There may still be silver-haired referees out there who award four points for a dropped goal, and who insist that the ball be played with the foot after a tackle. There is certainly no shortage of players who still believe in claiming a mark by whacking their heel into the ground. You might think the moral of this is 'Leave well alone', and you'd be right; but that won't stop me putting forward three law changes which I believe would improve the game. One is slightly bizarre and therefore stands no chance of ever being adopted. The other two are pure commonsense and therefore stand no chance of ever being adopted.

My first change would bring back the Field Goal.

The field goal was an exciting piece of enterprise, every bit as skilled as the dropped goal. It survives in American football: the ball is snapped back, a holder places it as a kicker runs up to kick at goal, and what makes it exciting is that all this takes place *during play*, so there are opponents doing their lively worst to interfere.

The fact that the International Board allegedly abolished the field goal in 1905 is neither here nor there. (The right of appeal to the referee was formally abolished in 1893, but that hasn't changed anything, has it?) Take a quick look at the current lawbook and you will see that there is nothing to stop a team scoring a field goal, and if the referee disallows it they should take him aside afterwards and show him Law 11, which defines a goal like this:

> A goal is scored by kicking the ball over the opponents' cross-bar and between the goal posts from the field-of-play *by any place kick* [my italics] or drop kick, except a kick-off, drop-out or free kick, without touching the ground or any player of the kicker's team.

No mention of the need to score a try or to be given a penalty kick before you can kick a goal. That means – since the laws allow whatever they don't forbid – that a goal can be scored without either of those formalities. All you need do to score a goal is place-kick (or drop-kick) the ball over the bar from the field of play. 'Any place kick', Law 11 says, and elsewhere the laws say 'a place kick is made by kicking the ball after it has been placed on the ground for that purpose'.

Suppose a team wins a scrum in front of their opponents' posts. Suppose the scrum-half passes back to his stand-off who instantly places the ball for the full-back to kick at goal. If he's on target, they've done everything the laws require to score a goal. There is one small obstacle. The laws don't give any points for a field goal. Penalty goal, dropped goal, goal from a try: yes. Field goal: zilch. Still, if you don't mention this to the ref he might give you three points for effort.

My second change concerns Law 10: Kick-off.

Ask yourself this question: what is the purpose of the kick-off? Quick as a flash, yet witty with it, you reply: 'To start the sodding game of course, you berk.'

And yet, does it? As often as not it *stops* the game. One of the most tedious features of modern rugby is the big boot at the kick-off that sends the ball bouncing through the in-goal and out of play. Two seconds after the start comes the stop. And that's nonsense.

It's done for a reason: the team kicking off wants to force a drop-out so that it gets offered the ball on the enemy 22. I don't care. The whole point of playing rugby is to *play* it. The founding fathers came up with a very fair and simple way of getting the game going, and for the best part of a hundred years the kick-off did its job. Then, in 1931, England were playing Ireland at Twickenham. Donald Burland, the Bristol centre, re-started the game after halftime by kicking the ball dead and forcing Ireland to drop out. This strange act drew much comment. It also inspired a lot of imitators. Burland has much to answer for. Kicking off dead is rugby's answer to soccer's long pass back to the goalkeeper. Both are boring evasions of the purpose of the game. The difference is that rugby is allegedly played for fun, and I believe it would be easy to increase the quantity of fun by adding just twenty-five words to Law 10:

> If the ball reaches touch-in-goal or the dead-ball line without first
> having been played by an opponent, a scrummage shall be formed
> at the centre.

Note that the team kicking off can still thump the ball over the goal-line if they want to. My change simply persuades them to make an effort to keep the ball in play. That's not a lot to ask, is it?

Before I announce my third change let me put another question to you. Are there too many penalty kicks in the game today? As I thought. In that case, here's a supplementary: do we want players to manufacture even more penalties when they could perfectly well avoid them?

What I'm driving at, in case you hadn't guessed, is the offside trap.

Whenever I see the ball held in the back row of a scrum while the scrum-half mimes grabbing it and dashes off with a dangerous look on his face and nothing in his hands, I let out a low moan, like a wounded fog-horn.

God knows there are enough stoppages in rugby already, and yet these players are doing their crooked best to make the other team get off-side so that the ref will be forced to blow up and give a penalty. The whole point of a scrum is to re-start play, to get both teams in action again. The offside trap kills that prospect at birth.

As far as I can tell, the man with the dubious honour of having invented the offside trap was Dickie Owen, Wales's scrum-half against England at Blackheath in 1902. England were leading 8-6 with only a few minutes left when Wales heeled at a scrum on the England 25 in front of the posts. As Owen told his forwards – in Welsh – to keep the ball in, he dummied his pick-up and pass. Oughtred, the English scrum-half, followed him and was off-side. Strand-Jones kicked the goal. Wales won, 9-8.

The rest is history, and fairly dreary history too, a lot of it, especially the last twenty years. The dismal spectacle of twenty-nine players standing around watching the thirtieth take his umpteenth longwinded pot at goal has become the norm, and – especially at international level – it is penalties, not tries, that decide games.

Well, the combined weight of the IB seems incapable of reversing that trend but there is no reason why the offside trap should continue to blight rugby with its bad acting. It could be abolished quite simply, by adding these lines to Law 8 (Advantage):

> The referee shall not whistle for an infringement when, in his opinion, the infringement has been intentionally brought about by the action of the non-offending side.

You might think that this places too great a responsibility on the referee. Not a bit. Any ref who can't identify the offside trap in a dense fog with one eye shut ought to retire immediately, and let the touch-judge finish the match. What's more, the laws already require the referee to decide when a team is faking or dummying in such a way as to lure the other side into getting into trouble. Law 28 (Free Kick) ends by warning: 'Neither the kicker nor a placer shall wilfully do anything which may lead the opposing team to charge prematurely. If either does so, the charge shall not be disallowed'. The Notes to that law tell the referee not to substitute a penalty for a free kick if he believes that the kicker's team deliberately contrived the penalty; and there's a similar Note to Law 27 (Penalty Kick), aimed at teams that try to fabricate a second penalty out of the first.

So there's no lack of precedent for telling referees to ignore any amateur dramatics whose sole aim is to stop the game and win a penalty for which the so-called non-offending side is really to blame. Indeed, the 'Objects of the Game' declare loud and clear that players should observe 'fair play according to the Laws and a sporting spirit'. Can it be fair play according to the laws when a team deliberately manoeuvres an opponent into breaking a law? No, it can't.

I've argued this point in many a clubhouse bar, and someone usually pokes me in the chest and says the offside trap is just a ploy, no different from selling a dummy, because both are intended to make the opponent go the wrong way; and besides, the offside trap is a way of keeping the opposing back row honest. They never know whether the ball is in or out, and that's worth a couple of yards to the team in possession.

All of which is true, as far as it goes, but it doesn't go far enough.

The difference between selling a dummy and working the offside trap is that the first aims to keep the game going while the second aims to bring it to a complete halt. Both are acts of deception, but what matters is their purpose. A team that fakes a pass to the blind side, then does a mis-move and dummy scissors before giving the ball to the wing who baffles the cover with a swerve and a sidestep – that team is out to deceive its opponents in order to score a try. If an opponent frustrates them by doing something illegal, that's too bad. They may get a penalty out of it, but that was not what they set out to do. They set out to play rugby. The team that uses the offside trap, on the other hand, isn't interested in playing rugby. It doesn't want to move the ball until it has stretched the defence to breaking-point. It wants to leave the ball where it is, between the number eight's size twelves, while its scrum-half auditions for RADA in the hope of getting three cheap points. The argument about keeping the opposing back row honest doesn't hold water. The referee will penalise them if they overstep the mark. When he does so, it will be because he wants to ensure that the team in possession gets a fair chance to use that possession.

The offside trap is not fair use of possession. The offside trap is the negation of rugby; and any player who uses it should be grilled over a slow fire while being forced to listen to 'Barry Manilow In Concert'. I have spoken.

On with the bawl

As I shuffle about the grubby underworld of rugby, where five consecutive passes count as a miracle and a dropped goal is an act of God, I've noticed a pattern of behaviour which leads me to make a sweeping statement.

This is that *the volume of noise produced in any match is directly converse to the degree of skill displayed.* Or, more shortly: *The dimmer, the louder.*

Now the odd thing about this is that the scrubby teams who make the most noise are invariably the ones who can least afford to waste their breath. They're so unfit that every syllable they utter takes another pace off their corner-flagging, which in any case is non-existent after the first ten minutes. Shouting is very tiring, as any pack-leader will tell you. So why do they do it?

Partly, it's because noise is a substitute for action in the lower orders of creation, such as farm dogs, women drivers and the members of the Extra B.

Farm dogs, for reasons best known to themselves, bay at the moon. Women drivers crawl along with the clutch half out and the engine screaming, under the impression that the noise is accomplishing something. And the Extra B shout at each other.

They exhort, they instruct, they denounce. None of it does the slightest good, because nobody is listening. Everybody is too busy shouting. You can't shout and listen at the same time, can you?

Another reason for all the noise is that arguing is infectious. If one idiot shouts out a load of old rubbish, and another idiot bawls back a load of contradictory rubbish, then idiot number three is at once incited to unload his own personal brand of bad advice, refuting them both. Otherwise he gets a guilty feeling that he's not doing his bit.

Anyone who has ever sat on a bad committee will know the sensation. When all the others have been talking tripe it is virtually impossible to remain silent — whether or not you have anything to say.

Now this is usually the point in the evening when some well-meaning old fogey comes up, refills your glass from the jug, and says: 'Never mind – as long as they enjoy themselves, that's the main thing,' before hobbling off in a haze of beer and self-deception.

The fact is that the game cannot be played properly if everybody talks all the time. It's no coincidence that a first-class match is almost completely silent, except for the captain and the pack-leader. The rest save their breath to run.

There is literally no time for discussion during a game of rugby. The ball moves too fast, and the bursts of play are too short – only ten or eleven seconds each. If the players don't know what to do, eleven seconds gives them no time to learn. Therefore, all the hubbub merely confuses a bloke who probably wasn't too confident in the first place. As they used to say in the Army: order, counter-order, disorder.

The deafening anarchy which you get in some games is the product of a sort of lunatic democracy which often infects low-grade rugby. The excuse for it is that every player should be free to have a go and do his best. After losing the toss, the captain ceases to lead his team, because he is afraid that they might resent any interference.

This is codswallop. Rugby is no more democratic than community hymn-singing. The need for a strong – in fact dictatorial – captain is greater at the bottom than at the top; the dunderheads need all the self-control they can scrape up, to compensate for their staggering incompetence.

If every Extra B skipper made his loud-mouths belt up and get stuck in, it would be a better game, and in the end they would enjoy it more.

If somebody won't belt up, you can always kick his legs from under him and jump on his stomach. There is nothing in the laws to say you mustn't strike a player on your own side, provided you don't obstruct an opponent while doing it.

If the captain won't make them shut up, then the ref should. Many refs don't, because it means stopping the entire game and lecturing the captains on their duties – and there's nothing in the laws about excessive chat.

But any ref who lets a game turn into a debate is asking for trouble. As I said before, you can't talk *and* listen at the same time, and with a chorus of thirty shouting the odds, the ref will have to blow his whistle like the one-o'clock hooter before anyone hears him.

If they still go on yakking, the chances are they won't hear what he has ordered – scrum, line-out, penalty, whatever. That means half of them get ready for the wrong thing. So he has to start again. They wander back, grumbling loudly. The game has ground to a halt, clogged by noise.

Apart from the harm they do to themselves, a noisy side often waste time, and this can damage their opponents' chances. Any dispute or misunderstanding which prevents the game from re-starting, also prevents the other side from getting on with it. No player has a *right* to question anything.

If he queries a penalty kick just when his opponents are trying to take a quick one and exploit a good attacking opportunity, he's really trying to deny them a fair advantage.

No player has the *right* to discuss anything. The captain may be *privileged* to ask the ref what went wrong, but nobody – rank and file or leadership – has the right to argue. It's bad for the game, and fatal for the arguers.

As Dr Almond, the man who was umpire for the first-ever international match (Scotland v England, 1871), used to advise referees: 'When in doubt, decide against the side that makes the most noise.'

The underground lawbook

I remember once going with a terribly keen referee to a game at some remote ground. The season had just started, and the referee took the captains aside to point out a change in one of the laws. He even gave them his new lawbook so that they could see for themselves.

The home skipper wiped his hands on his shorts and held the book by its edges, as if it were a snapshot of someone's new baby. Then he gave it back.

'Thanks very much,' he said, looking across at his team of eleven forwards and three full-backs, 'but I don't think it'll make all that much difference to us.'

He was right, of course. The lawbook describes an ideal game, not one played by a team which includes five sub-normal hookers (two of them operating outside the pack) on a field inaccurately marked out for hockey last season.

Yet there are thousands of teams like that, all somehow managing to make a game of it. Perhaps it would help if we had a second lawbook – a sort of underground lawbook – only for these teams.

For instance, Law 1 goes on about how the field should be marked out with lines and flags, and Law 6 says quite baldly: 'There shall be two touch-judges for every match.'

What the underground lawbook would do is advise how to handle the situation when the lines have been submerged under a sea of pasture, the flags have been pinched, smashed or used to light the boiler, and if either team possessed a touch-judge he'd be out there playing in the back row, which at present is non-existent.

Some years ago I reffed a match with no lines, flags, touch-judges, or (at one end) crossbar. It wasn't a great game, but it kept thirty drinkers off the streets for an afternoon.

'Look here, you lot,' I said at the start, 'you tell me when you're in touch, and I'll tell you when you've scored. The first bloke to complain can have the whistle, with my compliments.'

That's democracy, see.

Law 4 goes on about Players' Dress, but that's no help when both teams turn up with the same colours (especially if it's white). Tell the home side to change? Futile, at 3.40 p.m. Cancel the game? Defeatism. The underground answer is to have each side play half the match stripped to the waist ('berserk', as the Vikings put it).

Law 3 defines the 'Number of Players'. A typical underground case-law would read something like this:

> *Question*. Four players on the visiting side are late because: (a) the home club provided misleading directions; (b) local inhabitants have sent them to a lacrosse festival; (c) the driver had a fight on this ground last year and isn't too keen to find it again. The time is now 4.10 p.m. What should be done?
>
> *Answer*. Kick-off with equal numbers. If the missing players turn up, you can increase both teams together.

This may smack of fair play to some people, but in my experience you've got to take drastic action to avoid a shambles. For instance, it's all very well for the law-book to say that the object of the game is to 'score as many points as possible', but what do you do in a match where Team A are leading 40-nil at halftime?

According to the book, you soldier on . Team B get thrashed 75-nil, Team A get bored, and the whole afternoon's a waste of time. The underground lawbook would handle it differently.

At halftime, the captains would scrub round the contest, shuffle both lots of players, deal out a new pair of teams, and play a sensibly-balanced second half. In other words, they'd take the result for granted and make a match of it.

The underground lawbook would also have a section on physical hazards in the playing area – seepage from broken sewers; protruding manhole covers; old brick foundations. Conventional referees tend to move play *away* from these things, in case someone falls over or into them; but long experience of underground rugby suggests a better solution.

The best place for an obstacle is right underneath a scrum. It's worth shifting a scrum twenty yards sideways in order to blot out a manhole cover, or a bit of broken concrete. Nobody ever ran *through* a scrum.

There are many other things on which an underground lawbook could advise. What to do when a spectator assaults a player who has/has not just fouled an opponent. What to do when a fifty-seven-year-old prop forward continually clings to his opponent in the line-out because, damn it all, you can't expect him to jump, not at his age, and he's got to do *something*.

What to do when a foreign player gets upset and slaps an opponent's face, just like Maureen O'Hara used to do in the movies (I saw it happen not so long ago). What to do when a player has to ref a match; after all, although his own team know all about his funny ideas of the laws, the other team don't.

What to do when a player is rolling drunk (this usually happens at Sevens tournaments, when Jugthumpers I get knocked out in the first round, rapidly sink five pints each, and then get called upon to provide a substitute for Jugthumpers II, who are by now into the semi-finals).

Yes, there's an obvious need for an underground lawbook. I can think of only one obstacle to the idea but unfortunately it's a fairly serious one, shared by the real lawbook: nobody would read it.

Any colour you like as long as it's white

Basil D'Oliveira, as far as I know, never played rugby. Nevertheless he played an interesting part in a large rugby controversy.

For the benefit of the younger fellahs out there, I should explain that D'Oliveira grew up in South Africa. He was a conspicuously talented cricketer but he was also conspicuously not white so he moved to Britain and in due course played for England. He played very well, both as a batsman and a bowler.

In the sixties, the MCC governed English cricket and the MCC picked the touring parties. England were due to tour South Africa in 1968–69. At the start of the 1968 season D'Oliveira seemed an automatic choice for England but as the

summer went by he lost form and was dropped from the team that was playing Australia. Then Prideaux couldn't play in the final Test, and D'Oliveira was recalled. He scored a century. England won.

The players to go to South Africa were announced and D'Oliveira was not one of them. Loud rumblings and grumblings were heard in the land. It was said, quite bluntly, that the MCC had weakened England's chances for fear of treading on South Africa's political toes. This was denied, and a selector went so far as to say that D'Oliveira had been considered primarily for his batting and the plain fact was that better batsmen were available.

Many people disagreed, and the flinging of over-ripe tomatoes at the MCC continued. All of a sudden, Cartwright dropped out of the touring party. Cartwright was a bowler. The MCC asked D'Oliveira to take his place, and the uproar registered ten on the Beaufort Scale. The South African government refused to believe that the MCC had not had its arm twisted by someone – they didn't know who, but it was obvious to them that the whole thing was a sinister conspiracy. Not that D'Oliveira's selection got the MCC off the hook in England: quite the reverse. The meaning that was widely extracted from it was that the MCC, giving in to pressure, had made the right decision for the wrong reason. In any case it didn't matter. Vorster, the South African prime minister, called D'Oliveira 'a political cricket ball' and said he wasn't welcome. If the MCC had dropped him again they would have been tarred and feathered. They had no option but to cancel the tour.

Their handling of the D'Oliveira affair had generated a vast amount of distrust, ill-feeling and resentment. It had made no friends in either country. And there was no cricket at the end of it.

In the summer of 1969, *The Guardian* published a half-page article by me, called *Who will be the rugby D'Oliveira?* This raised a point that I thought had been overlooked in all the debate about sport and apartheid. There were several first-class coloured players in the British game: Ponsford Benka-Coker of Rosslyn Park, John Coker of Harlequins and Surrey, Keith McIntyre of Wasps. McIntyre was a Trinidadian. He was good enough to captain Middlesex, and he couldn't have been far from an England trial. And that, I thought, was where things got interesting:

> 'If he does (get a trial) the selectors must be conscious of the fact that, by giving him an opportunity to win an international cap, they may find themselves with a coloured player who is good enough to be a Lion; and this may force a showdown with South

Africa. It is an obvious possibility. And – human nature being what it is – people are bound to suspect that for this very reason good coloured players are not getting the recognition they deserve.'

Frank Wilson, the Cardiff winger, was a case in point. Wilson was black and when Cardiff toured South Africa he was not in the party. Perhaps selection was made entirely on merit; but the thought must arise that Cardiff avoided any conflict by not including Wilson. That may be an unworthy thought, but . . .

'The important thing to remember is that the damage is done even if the selectors are, in fact, completely honest and fair. The *suspicion* of bias can be just as destructive as the fact.'

When I wrote that article I was trying to focus attention not on the wider moral aspects of apartheid (which had had a pretty full airing) but on the narrow question of the wellbeing of British rugby. We'd all seen what a mess the MCC had got itself into, and I thought we should learn from it:

'It's only a matter of time before British rugby has its own D'Oliveira. We may as well start facing that prospect and deciding where we stand. It's not just a question of how we can get along with South Africa; it's a question of how we are going to live with ourselves.'

The publication of the article made me very few friends in the rugby establishment. (I wrote it originally for the magazine *Rugby World*, to which I contributed regularly, but the editor rejected it. *Rugby World* didn't believe in rocking the boat.) The *Guardian* article appeared in October 1969, before the arrival of the Springboks on the tour that was harassed and disrupted by the 'Stop The Seventies Tour' campaign. I was naive enough to believe that I might be doing British rugby a bit of good by alerting people to the risk of another D'Oliveira affair. It seemed to me that, from sheer self-interest, the men who ran British rugby should face up to this possibility. Instead, I found myself treated with grave suspicion. There were those who believed that I was creating difficulties where no real difficulties existed, and they wished heartily that I would shut up.

So strong was this response that I wondered, briefly, if they might be right. Then I learned of the experiences of two men, and I knew they were wrong.

One man was Billy Boston. His father was Puerto Rican and his mother was Welsh. Even as a boy in Cardiff, where they're not easily impressed by rugby

Billy Boston, Cardiff-born and one of the best postwar wing-threequarters – but the wrong colour for a Lions tour to South Africa. Rugby Union's loss was Rugby League's gain.

prodigies, he was an outstanding wing-threequarter. He played for the Welsh Boys' Clubs and for Wales Youth. In the early 1950s he did his national service in the Army and scored six tries in the Army Cup Final. Billy Boston was big and strong and clever and very, very fast. He was odds-on to get a full Welsh cap, which would have put him in the reckoning for the 1955 Lions tour of South Africa.

But of course he wasn't white. Would the Welsh Rugby Union select him and thereby risk an eventual showdown with South Africa? It seems unlikely, and in any case Boston didn't wait to find out. He signed for Wigan Rugby League in 1953 at the age of nineteen. Next year, after only six professional matches, he was picked to tour Australia and New Zealand with the Great Britain Rugby League side. (Boston wasn't the first Welsh coloured player to go north to start his international career: Roy Francis, Colin Dixon and Clive Sullivan all made the same choice.)

Boston, at the age of twenty, scored a British record of 36 tries on that 1954 tour. In 1957 he went on a second tour. The British team arranged to play some exhibition matches in South Africa on their way home. There were two conditions. Boston would have to eat and sleep at separate hotels, away from the other tourists; and there must be no mention of him in the souvenir programmes. The British Rugby League authorities agreed. Boston, to his credit, did not. He came home alone.

It is hard to believe that, purely on merit, Boston would not have played for Wales and the Lions; but we shall never know. In the case of the other man there can be no doubt. George Nepia had already been on two All Black Tours – one to Australia, and one to Britain with Cliff Porter's 1924 Invincibles. He had played in every match on that tour and was second-top scorer with 77 points. Wavell Wakefield, then captaining England, said Nepia was 'the best full-back I have watched or played against since the War . . . His perfect catching of the ball, his kicking and his amazing power of breaking up a forward rush by whipping the ball off the ground and charging backwards into and through the oncoming forwards marked him out as a the player of a generation.' And Nepia was only nineteen at the time.

He was also a Maori. Many years later (in *I, George Nepia*, published by Herbert Jenkins in 1963) he wrote about the way that this simple fact affected his career; and how, in effect, South Africa told New Zealand which All Blacks not to pick:

> 'It is not perhaps generally known that until a late hour of 1927, at the end of which the All Blacks who were to tour South Africa in the following year were chosen, Jimmy Mill and I were strong candidates for the team. Not until the eleventh hour was it decided by the New Zealand Rugby Union that it would be impolitic for us, as non-Caucasians, to attempt to travel in a country whose policies towards non-Whites were even then severely restrictive.
>
> 'Mill and I, you may be sure, did not cry ourselves to sleep over this decision. Unhappily, this is an issue which has grown in importance, and from pride of race, if for no other reason, I am compelled to discuss it.
>
> 'I have already made mention of how the country was scandalised by the publication, the day after its despatch, of the message which the correspondent, Blackett, sent to his newspaper in South Africa about the match between the Springboks and the New Zealand Maoris at Napier in 1921. Putting aside all of the moral issues involved in the actual fact of publication in New

*A good man to have behind you: George Nepia, one
big reason why the 1924 All Blacks were invincible.*

Zealand, I feel bound to say that the sentence, "Bad enough having
to play team officially designated New Zealand natives but spectacle thousands Europeans frantically cheering on band of coloured men to defeat members of own race was too much for
Springboks who frankly disgusted", provoked a reaction and
bitterness which within the heart of the Maori race have neither
been forgotten nor forgiven.

'The omission of Mill and myself from the 1928 team was a
deliberate and conciliatory act by the New Zealand Rugby Union.
So was the decision not to commit the New Zealand Maori XV
against the Springboks who toured New Zealand in 1937. By
1949, when we were again to send a team to South Africa, the New
Zealand union had reaffirmed its policy and the Maori people,
much influenced by their greatest player of the time, the superb

midfield back, J. B. Smith, who agreed with the decision, said nothing. By 1956, when the Third Springboks visited New Zealand, it was judged safe to play the Maoris against them but so apprehensive were some officials of a racial conflict that the Maori team took the field brainwashed of any normally aggressive Rugby attitudes and were very thoroughly beaten. So it was not until 1959, and under a Pakeha [a non-Maori "Pakeha" has come to mean a white New Zealander] leader at that, that the Maoris really made known their dislike of the New Zealand union's intention not to consider Maori players in the selection of the team which was to visit South Africa in the following year.

'It is true that the protests which were made then, and again in the early months of 1960, tended to become tinged with radical politics. It is also true that among those who protested were Pakehas who were using us as a race for the purpose of pushing the kind of politics we as a race would not touch with a barge pole. Nevertheless, on many a marae throughout the country, there was a responsible opposition to the decision. In the years since 1921, the world had seen the deplorable effects of apartheid applied by successive South African Governments and culminating in the deplorably restrictive attitudes of the Afrikaner Nationalist Governments of Dr Malan, Mr Strydom, and Dr Verwoerd. As non-Caucasians, coloured folk if you like, we Maoris disliked this treatment of the millions whose skins were the same colour as ours. Most of all, perhaps, we were saddened, disappointed and humiliated by the attitude of the body, namely the New Zealand Rugby Union, which purported to be our guide, philosopher and friend. If you look down the years of organised Rugby in New Zealand, you will be struck by the importance the Maori segments assumes in affairs, not only in quality of leading players but also in actual numbers of participants. It is, as only one example, an indisputable fact that on a comparative basis, far, far more Maoris play Rugby up to a senior club level than do white men. Willingly, consistently, with the enthusiasm which I have tried to demonstrate in the previous chapter, the Maoris have given their loyalty to the game and to the controlling authority of the game.

'Loyalty begets loyalty, so they say. I wonder. My charge is that the New Zealand union, at this vital hour of challenge, sidestepped its obligations to us, the Maori people, for reasons that do not stand examination. There was a feeling of courtesy – which I would say was misplaced – towards the wishes of our South African hosts; there was the honouring of an obligation to the South African Rugby Board, which overlooked a much older, closer obligation to Maori Rugby and to the Maori race as a whole; and there was a fear of the consequences – international, sporting and financial – of a cessation of tours between South Africa and New Zealand. The New Zealand union's profit from the tour of the '56 Springboks was about £98,000 and the provincial unions which staged matches benefited to a comparable degree. In the final analyses, we Maoris, or very many of us Maoris, considered that the union had put aside the reciprocal loyalty which they owed to us for the sake of the profits they could see forthcoming from the 1960 tour and all subsequent tours between the two countries.

'I think we have won, all the same. Fortified by some inspiring political leadership, Pakeha and Maori of the New Zealand race have in the years since 1960 moved more steadily toward that state which was described by Governor Hobson at the signing of the Treaty in Waitangi in 1840 in the memorable phrase, "Now we are one people". In that state, I do not think we, as New Zealanders, will permit our New Zealand Rugby Union to maintain Rugby relationships with South Africa until and unless the South Africans accept us, Maori and Pakeha, as indeed one people. I marched for that concept at a protest in Wellington before the 1960 tour. So did many Maoris; and many Pakehas. We were one people. In the main business of living, as in Rugby, we must always be so.'

The milk train versus the express

One of the more enduring and endearing myths of the game is that Richard Burton had a trial for Wales. (Another legend is that Eamonn de Valera, first President of Eire, once played for Ireland.) But Burton grew up in Port Talbot, where his local club was (and is) Aberavon, and he wrote a nice piece about a game he saw in the thirties, when Cardiff were the visitors. Aberavon's usual full-back had been injured, so Police Constable Mog – for Morgan – Hopkins came out of retirement. To make matters more interesting, an ex-Aberavon player was in the Cardiff side: Arthur Bassett, capped by Wales at wing-threequarter. And at one stage in the game, Bassett got the ball near his own goal-line – or, as Richard Burton saw it, ninety yards from the other goal-line, with nothing between Bassett and a try but the Aberavon full-back:

> 'Except that Mog, having watched the match rather idly from a distance, for Aberavon had pursued Cardiff with such relentlessness that he had hardly been called upon to touch the ball or put foot to it all the afternoon, wasn't there. He was having an amiable chat with somebody in the crowd. With the great moan from the throng and all the instinct that is part of a great player, he realised that he was dressed up for something other than arranging to go to the Grand Hotel for sausages and mash after the match.
>
> 'He started to move like slowly gathering lumber. Bassett was going like venom out of a cobra and knowing perhaps that his old friend Mog had slowed down, he made the error of swerving in towards him, in order for him to swerve outside him with his superb acceleration, perhaps out of a feeling of superiority though I'd like to think not, but Mog Hopkins knew that if he could get to the points before they changed, he could stop the Express.
>
> 'It was for me a few seconds ripped out of eternity.

'One had the impression of TNT moving in one direction and slow-burning gun-powder in the other. It was a parabola of exquisite mathematics. Would the two curves meet? My stomach turned into warm water. Would the thickening milk-train catch the lean express? Pure mathematics could never have stopped Bassett, but pure mathematics is a kind of poetry, and like poetry depends on the human personality. And involved here were human personalities.

'Einstein proved that the shortest distance between two points was a curve. Bassett believed him. Hopkins was old-fashioned and believed with Euclid and Pythagoras that the shortest distance between him and Bassett was a straight line.

'The straight line destroyed the curve. Just in front of the old grand-stand Mog caught the great Bassett. Only barely. I mean very barely. Only by one ankle. But he caught him.

'It was a moment of great triumph. My stomach turned back into muscle and intestines and the warm water had turned cold.

'My mind may play me tricks and I am sure that Mr Bassett and Mr Hopkins and Mr Wooller will accuse me of distorted memory, but I prefer my memory of the truth to the truth itself.

'Because of that moment I have virtually forgotten everything else about the match.

'Who won?'

That way madness lies

Seven-a-side rugby is a subversive game. It takes a quiet, contented prop forward, puts the ball in his hands – *in his hands*, mark you – for perhaps only the second time in his playing career, and encourages him *to run with it.*

The shock to his system can be something diabolical. The man emerges from the game in a state of psychological shambles, totally confused.

I know about prop forwards, see, because I was one, so I understand how they (if they'll pardon the expression) think.

For a start, they don't want to have anything to do with that bunch of nancies behind the scrum – the fly-half standing on one leg and picking his cuticles; the centres, hands on hips, telling each other how nice their hair is; and the wings, who are getting on with their knitting.

No; prop forwards are well aware that all the important work takes place in the scrum. They might spare a word for the scrum-half, but even so it will be a short, squat word, the colour of khaki and covered in flies. The front row of the scrum is a closed community.

That being so, prop forwards take only a marginal interest in events outside the scrum. They lift their heads to note the spot where that daft propagator in the backs has knocked-on yet again, and then they set course for the comfort and security of another scrum, where they know they will be wanted and appreciated and hacked violently about the shins by people who talk their language.

Sevens shatter this pattern.

When your average prop forward turns out for Sevens, he suddenly finds himself virtually alone on a field slightly smaller than Heathrow Airport. By squinting, and shielding his eyes with his hand, he can make out the other players, but they are far, far away, often as much as ten or twelve yards apart. He feels naked, indecently exposed.

They kick off and sooner or later he gets the ball. This is when the psychological damage is done. Instinct urges him to put his head down and seek out the nearest ruck, but he can see that they haven't got anywhere near the quorum for rucks, so for a moment he panics.

Everything seems to go round and round, the blood rushes from his head, and he sways and totters. Then the mists clear from his eyes and he hears distant cheering. He realises that, entirely by accident, *he has just sold a dummy*. He starts to run, knowing that life can never be the same again.

And so another good man goes down to ruin. It's much the same for the threequarters, I suppose – they go out to play Sevens with their nails all polished and their aftershave tingling, and four minutes later they're having a right old ding-dong in the middle of a little old maul – but I always say that threequarters are easy to come by compared with a reliable prop who's been regularly cleaned and drained and wiped down with an oily rag.

I don't want you to think that prop forwards have a dull, reactionary influence on the game; quite the contrary. A case-history from my own club – Manhattan RFC – bears this out. You might not believe it, but it actually happened.

It concerns five prop forwards who were putting out the flags for a game. (Don't tell me there are only two props in a team; I've played in games where prop forwards formed a majority of those present.) They noticed a pebble or small stone on the pitch, and decided to remove it.

After a certain amount of hacking, they realised that the stone must be bigger than it looked, and they fetched spades. Digging revealed a large rock or small boulder. At the cost of considerable effort they eventually removed it. They now had (a) a large rock and (b) an even larger hole. Informed observers were quick to point out that play would be impossible with a cavity that size in the middle of the pitch. The five props held a short meeting, and reached an inspired decision.

They dug the hole a bit deeper, put the boulder back, and buried it. The game kicked off two and a half hours late. Three of those five props were Ph.D.'s, but I don't think that made much difference. Props are born, see, not educated.

Thud and blunder

'There are three kinds of Irish football,' wrote a Victorian sportsman. 'The first is the game where you kick the ball; the second, where you kick the man if you cannot kick the ball; and the third, which is purely Gaelic and most popular, where you kick the ball if you cannot kick the man.'

Rugby pundits have always been good at leaning over the fence and identifying dirty play in other countries, never in their own. They are usually suckers for the Golden Age, too. 'Rugby was never like that in my day,' they say. 'We played hard, but there was none of this dirty stuff you see today. Well, not much, anyway.'

I wonder. I suspect that rugby has always been a story of Beauty and the Beast. It's a story that rugby writers are sometimes reluctant to put in print, for very understandable reasons: when Brian Price, who captained Wales in the late sixties, read a report that clearly fingered him as the cause of the trouble in a match of thud-and-blunder, he sued and he won. But whenever two or three rugby writers are gathered together – say, at the bar of an Intercity express as they return from reporting a big game – they usually end up swapping opinions about who are the really hard men of the game: the men who are not only willing but eager to use fist or boot, knee or elbow, in order to slow down the opposition.

To join in these conversations is to get a startling view of some famous players, and of some famous clubs, too. Some of the most genial figures are shown to have a psychopathic streak; some of the most historic clubs turn out to be defenders of a tradition of winning at all costs. I remember covering an important match that opened with three brawls in quick succession. When the third fight began, several players ran ten or fifteen yards – not to separate the combatants but to join them; until a dozen men were slugging each other. Spontaneous combustion I could understand, but not this rush to stoke the fire before it went out. A fellow-reporter, a man who had played a lot of top rugby, put me straight. 'I came here four years in a row, on tour,' he said, 'and I never saw the end of a match. I got carried off each time. Unconscious.'

So why do they go on playing? One answer is that sometimes they don't. The players' ultimate sanction is to scrap the fixture. Believers in the Golden Age school of thought should note that this was not unknown in the good old days. In Edwardian times, for instance, Newport–Llanelli meetings became so violent that, after an especially brutal match in 1910, Newport called the whole thing off. (At the same time Llanelli sued a Newport newspaper for libel. The paper's report of the game had been too frank, and Llanelli won. However, the court took a realistic view of the harm done to Llanelli's reputation, awarded damages of one farthing, and ordered the club to pay costs of over £5000; so it turned out to be an expensive fit of righteousness.) Another club that occasionally ran short of opponents was Neath. Neath wear an all-black strip, which they adopted as a mark of respect after a forward was killed during a match with Bridgend. The incident did not noticeably alter Neath's approach to the game, which consisted largely of selecting men who felt no pain and instructing them to take no prisoners. It was grim, grinding stuff, and more than one club decided to do without the pleasure of Neath's company. As late as the 1960s, Cardiff – after a visit by Neath had generated more heat than light – instituted divorce proceedings; and it was four years before they got together again. Not that Welshmen have a patent on intimidation. English clubs – notably Gloucester and Coventry – have in their time had reputations for leaving their scruples with their teeth, in the dressing-room.

In 1983 the experienced Moseley prop, John Davidson, was told that his rugby career was finished after his jaw and cheekbone had been broken by a blow from a Swansea player. He considered taking legal action, but dropped the idea when Swansea disciplined the player (without naming him). Davidson said: 'On the club circuit in England and Wales there are roughly a dozen players whom I'd describe as psychopathic thugs. I don't think that's going over the top. In the context of what happened to me, that description is not too strong.' (Later, after three operations, including the insertion of a plate, Davidson learned that he could, in fact, play again.)

Two events in the winter of 1978 prompted a public debate about dirty play that went far beyond the sports pages: the tearing open of Chris Ralston's scalp by somebody's boot in a ruck during the Richmond–Llanelli game in November, and the stamping on J. P. R. Williams's face in a ruck during the Bridgend–New Zealand match in December. Ralston needed more stitches (thirty-two in all) but JPR's injury got more publicity because it was frighteningly close to his eye and because millions saw it happen on television.

Wilf Wooller – an outstanding centre and captain for Wales in the thirties – blamed the damage on a win-at-all costs attitude, the product of a coaching system that was too professional and too powerful. In the thirties, he said, forward play was 'tough, often rough and uncompromising, but the boot was not an approved weapon . . . ' He quoted the words of his first Welsh captain, Watcyn Thomas:

> 'If there is something dark on the ground, and it moves, kick it. It might be the ball. If it is dark and still, stand on it. It might also be the ball. If it squeals, say sorry.'

Wooller made it clear that this advice was facetious. Thomas had gone further and claimed that it was mythical. He said there was no truth in an English newspaper report that he had delivered the following pep-talk before the 1933 England–Wales match:

> 'If you see a dark object on the ground, kick it, it might be the ball; or tread on it, and if it squeals, say "Sorry, old chap" and carry on.'

Whether it was real or invented; serious, funny, or a bit of both, we shall never know; but it is interesting to compare it with something that happened to Wavell Wakefield when he was captaining the Harlequins in the 1920s:

> ' . . . during a club game at Twickenham I came upon two opposing forwards putting the boot, as I thought, rather unnecessarily hard

into one of our players. I went up and gently remonstrated, when one of them turned and in a most surprised voice said, "Good Lord, Wakers, we thought it was you we were kicking, or we shouldn't have been doing it!" – a most diplomatic remark!'

But boots are not the only extremities that can be put into an opponent unnecessarily hard. Knees can also be used – indeed the All Black coach Jack Gleeson said of the match in which JPR was trampled that in the very first scrum, Bridgend knees were battering the New Zealand front row. Teeth are another weapon. When Geoff Frankcom, the Cambridge and (later) Bath centre, won his first cap for England against Wales in 1965, there were prominent bite marks on his body after the match, and Frankcom had no doubt which Welsh forward's teeth would fit the marks. A few years later, an Australian hooker on tour in England went further and bit off part of an opponent's ear. Even by Australian standards that sort of thing was considered excessive and the management sent him home.

No doubt the Australian hooker had reason for his moment of cannibalism, just as the All Black Ken Gray had reason for breaking Jeff Young's jaw during the New Zealand–Wales match at Christchurch in May 1969. Wales were never in the game (New Zealand won 19-nil) and the All Black pack was dominant: at one stage they won sixteen rucks in succession. Wales grew desperate. Young pulled too many jerseys. Gray got exasperated. Exit Young. Nobody got sent off, just as nobody had been sent off two months earlier in the Wales–Ireland game that became known as The Battle of Cardiff Arms Park. It began with ten minutes' sporadic thuggery, and then Brian Price hit Noel Murphy. It was a right uppercut that started somewhere around the Welsh Captain's knees and lifted Murphy off the ground before it left him flat on his back. Price explained later that hostile fingers had been clawing at his eyes; he didn't know who they belonged to but he'd had enough of them.

The following year, Ireland made a short tour of Argentina and lost both international matches. They also lost a fair bit of blood. One prop from each team was sent off in the first international, which the Irish captain called 'the most savage match I have ever seen'. I believe him, and I'm not at all sorry I missed the spectacle. I saw the match between Western Counties and Fiji, also in 1970, and that was more than enough for me.

It was a strange day.

The weather was dank and grey but the crowd pouring into the Kingsholm ground at Gloucester was fizzing with universal good cheer. Eighteen thousand people had paid to see the Fijians and they were all looking forward to an afternoon of exuberant, irreverent, hell-for-leather rugby. Fiji had made a dazzling tour of Wales a few years earlier, and now the RFU had had the happy idea of inviting them to celebrate its centenary season. They began by galloping past Devon and Cornwall, 3-17, in typically carefree style, and now – just to add spice to the feast – they were to play Somerset and Gloucestershire on the very day that Fiji was attaining its independence.

They ran out to a tremendously happy roar. Kingsholm crowds are not easily impressed, but they had a welcome for this team from a scattering of islands on the far side of the world: islands with fewer than half a million people, yet able to create free-running, high-scoring rugby that, at its best, could challenge the might of New Zealand and Australia. Everyone there *wanted* a memorable afternoon. We got one, but not the way we expected.

I may have been one of the few people to suspect that something was wrong before the kick-off. I wanted to arrange a post-match interview with the Fijians' coach, so I tapped on their dressing-room door and went in.

Nobody looked up. Nobody spoke. Hardly anyone moved. It was like the grave in there. For the first time in my life, I tip-toed across a rugby dressing-room. Their coach was hunched over a guitar, fingering an occasional melancholy chord. In a whisper, I introduced myself and made my request. He nodded, once, sombrely. I tip-toed out, past the motionless players with their massive, brooding faces, and softly shut the door.

Brother, I said to myself, *that is not a happy team.*

The Fijians had let it be known that they were determined to win this Independence-Day game. Western Counties, however, were led by David Rollitt, the England flanker. Rollitt was not a good loser; indeed, in his own words, he was the world's worst loser. It wasn't so much a game of rugby as a collision of wills, of styles, of bodies.

It would be silly to think that the Fijians started all the rough stuff. But if the intimidation was mutual, the reactions were widely different. Western Counties remained disciplined and organised while the Fijians became angry, reckless and finally demoralised.

They were five points down in no time. We expected the unorthodox, but a long throw-in at a line-out near your own goal is plain daft. The Fijians' gloom deepened as they suffered a salvo of penalty kicks, most of them for technical offences which, it was clear, they found utterly unrecognisable.

Only twice in the first half did they succeed in cutting loose. The first break took them the length of the field, with backs and forwards slinging the ball about like demon jugglers, and a fifteen-stone prop, Qoro, side-stepping over the line to score. In the second break, Batibusaga at fly-half – who ran the way his name sounds – ricocheted through the defence. He converted both tries, but Counties, with a penalty and a dropped goal, led 11-10 at the interval.

The crowd had begun by cheering everything the Fijians did. Now there was a feeling of disenchantment. The great occasion had turned sour. Briefly, Batibusaga put Fiji in the lead with a neat dropped goal, but they soon threw it away when a foolish knock-back gave Hannaford a try. After that the slog went on, grimly exhausting. Towards the end the Fijians began to lose hope, and Western Counties steadily tightened their grip. John Gabitass kicked a long penalty (via the crossbar); then a short one; and finally he added a try and a conversion – eleven points in fifteen minutes.

So Western Counties won, 25-13. It was a sad victory. Fiji were booed off the field. We learned that Gabitass had a fractured cheekbone. John Pullin, the Counties' hooker, was already in the dressing-room, a trail of surgical thread around his nose, over his right eye, at the back of his skull – fifteen stitches in all.

His prop, Tony Rogers, had a broken nose. Scrum-half John Spalding was nursing battered ribs. Everybody was cut, bruised and aching. The referee had played a total of nearly twenty minutes' injury time.

Well, rugby is a hard game, and the Fijians are a tough lot; but they are not as huge as many people think. Behind the scrum that day they averaged 5ft 8in and 12st 4lb; and the biggest forward on the field was Bristol's David Watt. So what had gone wrong? What had turned the exuberance into recklessness, and the joyful abandon into something dangerously near savagery? I think there were three causes.

First, the Fijians were genuinely bewildered by many of the referee's decisions, and they began to despair of ever doing *anything* right.

Second, the Fijians's extrovert style of play tends to bring their knees and elbows into action with unusual vigour – which, although it may have explained why an opponent got a wallop in the ribs, still didn't make him feel any happier about it.

Third, it was their Independence Day, and they were a long way from home. They missed their tour manager, Ratu Ganilau, son of a hereditary chief, and a lieutenant-colonel who won a DSO while fighting terrorists in Malaya. Normally, Ratu Ganilau kept the lads in line, but that day he was back in Fiji for the ceremonies.

'And when they are like this,' their coach told me sadly, 'there is nothing I can do.' Perhaps that was why he had been playing his guitar; perhaps it took his mind off what was coming.

That was in 1970. A year later the Lions elevated violence to an art form with their theory of getting your retaliation in first, and thus was launched a fairly dirty decade. The second Test in England's tour of Australia in 1975 saw Mike Burton become the first English player to be sent off in an international. This happened only minutes after the start, but there was enough open warfare in those few minutes to justify sending off a dozen men. In 1977 it was Wales v Ireland again: the Celts v the Gaels: Geoff Wheel (Swansea) v Willie Duggan (Blackrock College), a heavyweight eliminator that succeeded only in eliminating both of them: the first players sent off during an international at Cardiff. When the sides met at Lansdowne Road in 1978 it was another bruising, bloodyminded clash. The fight for possession in rucks and mauls was more than fierce: it was frightening. 'At this rate,' one of the Welsh players said afterwards, 'somebody's going to get killed.' That summer, Wales followed England's example and made a short tour of Australia. They enjoyed it no more than England had done. Three minutes after the start of the second Test, someone hit Graham Price slightly harder than Brian Price had hit Noel Murphy, and broke his jaw in two places. There was a general punch-up in progress at the time, and Price's attacker played out the match.

He was named as Steve Finnane by an observer, the Welsh international referee Meirion Joseph. He condemned Australia for picking Finnane to tour New Zealand after the foul on Graham Price. Joseph named a few more names while he was at it: Ray Gravell for 'lack of discipline' in the first Test against Australia; Gerard Cholley, the French prop, for laying Donald MacDonald with a punch in the France–Scotland match of 1977; J. P. R. Williams for late-tackling Mike Gibson in the Ireland–Wales match, also of 1977 (a sad lapse by JPR, that: he deliberately conceded the penalty-kick rather than allow Gibson to exploit an attacking opportunity). Meirion Joseph could afford to get it all off his chest, because in the summer of 1978 he retired at the early age of forty-one in protest at the mounting violence in the game.

'Dirty rugby has become so commonplace,' he said, 'that I decided I simply didn't want to referee any more.' There was considerable debate about that. There was no argument two years later when Wales played England at Twickenham. 'It was war on the field and like M*A*S*H in the medical room,' Leon Walkden, the RFU's honorary doctor, reported. He put a total of twenty-two stitches into Colclough, Beaumont, Smith and Scott. His Welsh counterpart sewed up Phillips, the hooker. Uttley went off hurt at halftime. And of course Ringer got sent off after fifteen minutes.

Before Ringer's departure, while the teams were still striving to prove Meirion Joseph dead right, one ex-international in the stand turned to another and said: 'Why don't we go and play squash? I didn't come here to see this.' It was indeed embarrassingly bad, so bad that it took much of the pleasure out of the rest of the championship. If that was what international rugby was all about, who cared which team won? In fact, international rugby seemed to hit bottom in the Ringer match; thereafter it had nowhere to go but up. But whether or not that particular game was the worst ever is a moot point. It would have to be worse than the match between Ireland and Wales at Belfast in 1914, and that was in a class of its own.

The best account of it came from a forward, Percy Jones of Newport:

> 'We had an early warning of the "rough house" that was in store for us. On the Friday night we went to a theatre, and Harry Uzzell, George Hirst and I sat together with a couple of the Irish team. Soon Dr Tyrrell, the leader of the Irish forwards, came across, and said: "Here, Uzzell; where's this Percy Jones you've got about with

Nothing personal, you understand, old chap. Two views of the England Trial of 1900, as seen by The Illustrated London News. *The maniac with the moustache, having seized one of his own team, is about to hurl him at the selectors.*

you? I'll have a go at him tomorrow." "All right," I replied. "I'm a Welshman, and I'll be with you." Then he said (and we were all quite pally about it): "Now Jones, it's you and me for it tomorrow!" "I shall be with you, doing the best I can," I said modestly.'

Next day conditions were perfect for a fight: half a gale of wind and rain lashing down in torrents. The rough-house began shortly after the kick-off:

> '... In the first few minutes Tyrrell got me, and everything inside my head rattled ... The next thing that happened was that M. Abraham, the Irish centre, kept "having a go" at me as well; and so I called Uzzell over, saying "You'd better come with me; there's another bloke at it now." After that we kept together, and the fun went merrily on ... At halftime, Tyrrell's estimate of the score was that he was "two up", and I agreed, "But you'll not be leading for long," I promised him.'

The conflict had spread outwards from Jones and Tyrrell. One of the pressmen, W. J. T. Collins, wrote of the forwards:

> 'Perhaps half of them played football, the others let themselves go with unrestrained roughness. The referee, a Scotsman, simply ignored it. Many of the fierce exchanges took place when his attention was engaged elsewhere. With the ball away in the hands of the threequarters, gentlemen in red and green jerseys who had been carrying on pleasant private conversations in the scrummage (or breathing threatenings and slaughters!) raised their heads and looked for someone with whom to continue the argument; and it was only out of the corner of the eye that we who were following the ball saw many of the clashes. But enough happened under the very nose of the referee and in full view of the press to justify the ordering-off of half a dozen players. Scores of times men were tackled and flung to the ground when they were yards from the ball; frequently blows were exchanged; there were times when the game was more like a free fight than scientific Rugby football. But this must be said – it was not malicious or bad-tempered. It was as if the men had agreed to an hour's "all-in football" to find out who could take the most punishment. The Irishmen made the discovery about halfway through the second half.'

As Percy Jones put it:

> 'Uzzell, who was leading our pack, decided that we should play them at their own game. And we did! The play that followed was easily the fiercest that I ever saw or took part in . . . It waxed hotter and hotter; there was no squealing, by us or them, and after the game, too, we were all the best of pals. But we soon had them beaten. Uzzell was saying "Come on! We've got them going now!" But they were gone! And even Tyrrell gave in at last. "You're the best Welshman I've ever run across," he said to me. "You are the only man who ever beat me" . . . The fiercest game that any of the thirty players had ever taken part in was followed by the friendliest dinner. Tyrrell and I sat together, and we signed each other's menu cards as a more permanent memento of the terrific struggle than the many bruises we had previously accepted from each other.'

It was 'fierce', it was 'rough', but was it dirty? With scores of late tackles and frequent exchanges of blows, could it be anything else? Was it even rugby? I leave that to you to decide. Incidentally, Wales won 11-3, and the Welsh captain was the Rev J. Alban Davies of Llanelli. Perhaps they selected him in case someone was needed to administer the last rites.

Of course the game was much tougher in my time

Well, people have been saying that ever since rugby was old enough to have started going downhill, which is what each succeeding generation says about it: rugby, like *Punch*, is never as good as it used to be. Or perhaps it's never as bad as it used to be, because the old-time giants of the game certainly seemed to be measured in terms of how many men they could eat for breakfast. Back in the days when shorts were long and only a cad would contemplate scoring a goal from a penalty kick, it was a very red-blooded game. You could tell that by looking at the grass afterwards.

One story gives us a kind of negative yardstick of early turn-of-the-century fortitude. D. D. Dobson was a distinguished England forward. He scored a try in his first international, against Wales in 1902, did the same thing next year, and won six caps in all. In 1916, when he was out in Nyasaland, he got knocked down and killed by a charging rhino. Eventually word reached his old school in Devon and the games master observed: 'Dobson always had a weak hand off.'

They liked their players to be titanic in those days. Harry Vassall had set the style, back in the 1880s. He was a thinker: under his leadership the Oxford University side was unstoppable for three years and his ideas revitalised the game. But it was his size that impressed. A friend said that Vassall was 'broader in the beam than any man I have ever seen'. Hacking was still the done thing in the scrums – strictly banned, of course, which meant there was a lot of it going on – and while taking tea and crumpets with his Oxford chums Vassall used to take off his plus-fours to display his collection of scars, all earned for the greater glory of University rugby.

Modern rugby is not without its hard men: Keith Murdoch, who toured Britain with the 1972 All Blacks, had that reputation. As a result he got more than his fair share of attention from the press until one day he picked up a reporter by the hair. After that they respected his privacy, or perhaps they had too much respect for their own hair. And Colin Meads, one of the greatest All Black locks, was not

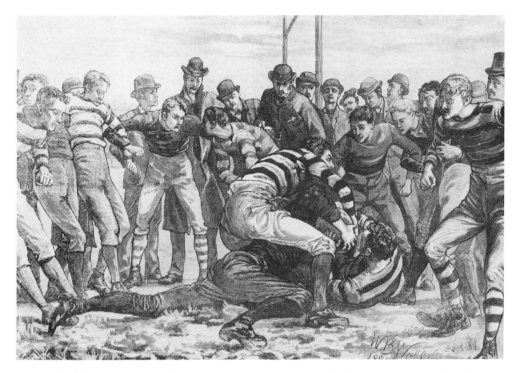

English club rugby, 1882. Note how opponents have linked arms to protect the players from the public, half of whom have thoughtlessly strayed on to the pitch.

called 'Pinetree' just because of his height. Being tackled by Meads was like having a tree fall on you. Off the field, however, Meads was an outstandingly gentle and generous man. I remember waiting to interview him in his hotel while he dealt with a small boy who wanted his autograph. The lad was very unathletic-looking: fat, dumpy, awkward, bespectacled, and he was very particular about getting Meads' signature on eight or nine books and magazines and programmes. Meads took endless care to be sure that his name was in the right place each time. There he stood like a great, grave totem-pole, unhurried, unflappable, courteous, while this scruffy, inky-fingered kid searched through a magazine for the exact action picture he wanted signed. Meads was the most patient man I have ever seen. Surprisingly he could also be deeply superstitious. He hated being captain because it meant leading the team out, and that, he was convinced, always brought bad luck. He came out first in South Africa, broke his arm in the match, and knew what to blame it on. What would have been a trifle to anyone else mattered enormously to this great man.

Someone who often played full-back with Meads was Fergie McCormick. He made a lot of tries by injecting his considerable presence into the backline. He was an expert at what's known as the Maori sidestep: he ran into, through and over the defender. But there's nothing new in rugby, and in the early twenties Ireland had a wing-forward called Jammie Clinch who also ran through opponents as if they were open doors. Meetings then between Ireland and Wales were not occasions for spectators of a nervous disposition. Jammie had fond memories of brisk encounters with Wales, and they remembered him too. One year Ireland went to Cardiff and as he ran onto the field he heard a Welsh voice shout: 'Send the bastard off, ref!' He took that as a great compliment.

Jammie went on the Lions tour to South Africa in 1924. He and Blakey Blakiston, the England flanker, became great friends. There's a story that Jammie had so much trouble with a Springbok that he lost his patience and flattened him. Blakey reproached him for not doing it more thoroughly. 'Look at him,' Blakey said, 'he's up again, ready for play!' Next year England were playing Ireland at Twickenham and Blakey got laid out. As his vision cleared he saw Jammie Clinch bending over him, looking anxious. 'Did I do it right that time, Blakey?' he asked.

Packing down on the other flank of that England scrum was another superb forward, every bit as good as the hooker Sam Tucker (27 caps) and the locks Wavell Wakefield and Cove-Smith (31 and 29 caps respectively). Tom Voyce played 27 times for England, and there's a marvellous photograph of the team taken before his first appearance, against Ireland in 1920. One or two players display modest smiles but most of them – drawn from the stiff-upper ranks of Blackheath, the Royal Navy, Cambridge and Harlequins – look dutifully stern. Tom was a Gloucester boy. He was tickled pink to be playing for England and his grin is as unruly as his hair. Wavell Wakefield, next to him, had parted his hair with a sliderule and beaten it into submission with a pair of silverbacked brushes. Tom Voyce's hair went its own blithe way, like its owner.

He was a magnificent flanker because he loved playing; he couldn't get enough of it; he wanted to do it all, tackle, run with the ball, pass, cover. He made a lot of tries for England and he took the legs from under a lot of opponents who thought they were past him. Nothing – except, eventually, age – slowed him down. In one especially abrasive game he turned his cheery, bloody face on his captain, Wakefield, who was just as battered, and said: 'Up with your sleeves, my old skip. By golly, it's real good fun, isn't it? I didn't know they went in as hard as this . . .' No matter how hard they went in they never dented Tom Voyce's enthusiasm.

He went on to become President of the Rugby Football Union. I remember him at the end of his life when he was virtually blind but he still attended every

Gloucester and Gloucestershire game if he could. Often he sat beside me in order to listen to the commentary I was doing for BBC radio. Tom Voyce enjoyed every moment that life had to offer.

It's a pointless but irresistible pastime to wonder how players of different ages would have got on if they'd faced each other. How would Jammie Clinch or Tom Voyce have tackled the Scottish wing-threequarter of the 1880s, W. E. MacLagen? 'If he got the ball within a dozen yards of the line,' wrote the game's historian, Marshall, 'he was a most dangerous man in more ways than one . . .' And although Marshall didn't reveal exactly what MacLagen did to ensure a score (a Gaelic sidestep, maybe?) he gave a hint when he told something of MacLagen's technique in defence. 'More than once he has tossed a man, full pitch as the bowlers would say, onto the little paling at Raeburn Place and made the timber crack.' Hmm. Reminds me of the tales about a New Zealand forward called Charlie Seeling, who toured Britain with the 1905 All Blacks. Seeling was famous for his dive-tackles; they were spectacular and – provided his timing was right – effective. On one occasion he got his timing wrong and hurled himself clean through a picket fence. He played on, of course. A few years ago, during a debate about the supposed decline of All Black rugby, an old player wrote to a New Zealand magazine: 'In my day, you only went off with a broken leg or if you were concussed.' You think he was exaggerating? In 1918 a Frenchman, M. F. Lubin-Lebrère, came back from the war with seventeen bullets in his body and only one eye. The doctors removed the bullets and he embarked on a career for France, playing in the second row. His only problem was unscrupulous opponents who clapped a hand over his good eye. And what about Watcyn Thomas, fourteen caps for Wales between the wars. Broke his collarbone after ten minutes, played on, and eventually forced his way over the line to score the winning try. With three opponents on his shoulders.

Or so they say.

Coaching, we're told, has ruined the game. Players have become programmed to follow set routines. Flair withers, and no bird sings.

It's true. The inspired improvisation, the brilliant flicker of unorthodoxy, has all but vanished. This is not to say that teams should go onto the field without any pre-planned moves, but rather that they should be ready to modify these moves under the pressure of events. That's what we did in all the teams I ever played for, and the results were full of surprise. So, in the interests of encouraging better, brighter rugby, I think the time is ripe to disclose the system of signals we used, together with a brief description of the meaning of each.

138

SPECIFIC TACTICS

Yours! Christ, that's a big fellah coming at me . . .

Mine! Where *is* everybody?

Scissors Let's you and me have a little private cock-up.

Dummy Scissors I'll keep going while you run into the referee.

Tapped Penalty Let's all of us have a great big public cock-up.

Loop Let's make the backs run sideways across the field, because the forwards need the exercise.

Miss-Move Sorry, it slipped.

Crash Ball Everyone else has knocked-on, so why not him?

Scissors plus Loop followed by Dummy Scissors with a Miss-Move as the fullback fakes a Dummy Crash Ball If we don't know what the hell we're up to, how on earth can they know?

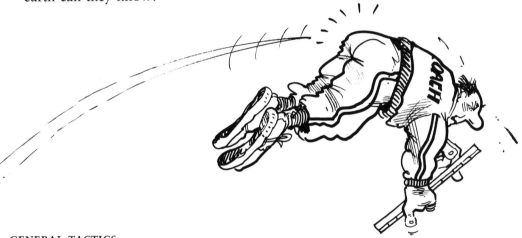

GENERAL TACTICS

Short Lineout Six of our pack are still throwing up on the other side of the field.

Keeping it Tight The scrum-half's drunk.

Second-Phase Possession Making off with your best friend's girl.

Third-Phase Possession Jesus, this is murder – they're even less fit than we are.

Fourth-Phase Possession Blow up, ref, for Christ's sake, I think I'm having a heart attack.

Garryowen Sorry, it slipped.

EMERGENCY TACTICS

Late Tackle I got there as soon as I could, ref.

Early Tackle I haven't got all afternoon to hang about, you know.

Hospital Pass Sorry, it slipped.

As far as I know, there is only one way for an ambitious young barrister, a rising accountant, or a personal assistant to the managing director to be able to turn up with a limp, a thick ear, and four stitches over the right eye, every Monday morning from early September to late April, without arousing adverse comment in the executive washroom; and that is to play rugby.

Many captains of industry and colonels of commerce actually approve of these sundry abrasions, as signs of dash, pluck, stamina and all those qualities which a young executive must have to elbow his way through the hurly-burly of modern business.

'Morning, Trubshaw!' they call out. 'Had a good game of rugger?' And when Trubshaw replies in the affirmative, speaking with some difficulty because of a split lip and a blinding hangover, they smile and mentally chalk him up for another thousand a year, little knowing that Trubshaw actually fell flat on his face while chasing a blonde down the cellar steps at a party which was eventually closed down by the police at three in the morning.

One of the things that makes rugby such an interesting game, from the psychiatric point of view, is this casual attitude to injuries. Provided the chap hasn't damaged anything vital (such as his drinking elbow), everybody treats his case as comic relief, justifying healthy laughter and allegations of malingering. (The French, who have a critical eye for melodrama, shout 'Cinèma!' at players who they think are piling on more agony than they actually feel.)

I began collecting injuries – other people's – the day I saw Cambridge University demolish a side so thoroughly that when one of the Cambridge forwards – a prop who looked like a cross between the Piltdown Man and the back of a bus – succeeded in scoring a try, they let him take the conversion kick. The game was almost over, anyway.

He gave a lot of thought to setting up the ball. Then he paced backwards, staring hard at the maker's name, and came to a halt. His chin sank slowly to his chest, like a lift reaching the basement, and his hands trembled as if releasing a dose of excess tension. He leaned forward, pounded down on the ball, drew back his leg, and stabbed his boot powerfully into the ground, sending a light spray of earth over the ball and shattering his ankle, so that two strong men had to carry him off.

The ball, I remember, still stood, a monument to unfulfilled ambition.

One of the sure-fire comedy injuries – the kind that has the spectators slapping their thighs and calling for more – is when the crossbar falls down and clouts a defender.

What usually happens is that a conversion or penalty kick hits a post and shakes the pins out, but an even more hilarious switch is for a defender to kick for touch from his in-goal and knock the crossbar down; then, while a bevy of defenders lie senseless between the uprights, an attacker dives on the rebound and scores. This is guaranteed to have the crowd falling about uncontrollably.

Nobody has yet seen a clobbered player crack a smile, however, just as nobody has heard a referee chuckle when a player collides with him as he inserts the whistle between the lips and abruptly finds it forced halfway down his gullet. It's much easier to grin and bear it when you do the grinning and somebody else has to have the stitches put in.

I've never found teams of medical students much help, either. If it looks like a dislocated elbow, they always say they haven't got to that bit yet, but, if it's any consolation, the patient's ear-nose-and-throat condition is satisfactory and he is in no danger of a heart attack. I remember one team of medical students who

couldn't tell cramp from croup; it turned out that fourteen were dentists and one was a vet.

Even if you have a bloke who knows his sporting medicine, the treatment can sometimes be as dangerous as the injury. A top referee told me of a game in which a player suddenly collapsed and began flinging his limbs around as if he had tarantulas in his pants. The ref called on a doctor who happened to be watching. This man took a shrewd, professional look and said: 'Do nothing.'

Reluctantly the team stood back while the victim revved his limb-flinging up into second gear and wound his eyeballs back to zero.

'It's just a fit,' said the M.D. 'Leave him alone.'

Within seconds, however, the body began to turn deep blue and make strange yodelling noises; and the team was about to assassinate the doctor for killing off not only their respected friend but also their only decent goal-kicker when the chap sat up and asked for a drink of water.

The whole incident, the ref said, was on a par with another occasion involving an Irish side, where one player collected a truly enormous cauliflower ear, and another player who was a doctor said that the only thing to do at all was to drain off the fluid as quickly as possible, d'ye see, so they gave the first fellah a tumberful of Irish whiskey and, while he wasn't looking, the captain punched his head and knocked him out. They drained all the fluid away before he came round but he had concussion for the next three weeks.

Then there was the case of the player who damaged a finger. As the first-aid case was in its usual ransacked condition, they splinted it with a teaspoon and his laces, and sent him off to hospital.

'What's the matter?' asked a medical student.

'I can't move my finger,' replied the player.

'No wonder,' said the student, 'you've got a damn great teaspoon tied to it.'

Stranger things have happened. I once saw an international wing play a blinder in a county match, right up to the moment when he went over to a line-out and the ten-year-old ball-boy hit him in the eye with the ball and laid him out.

And I myself once had an anti-tetanus shot before playing Sevens in New York, on a field which had just been used for a polo tournament. It wasn't the discarded horseshoes we worried about so much as the fresh manure. That stuff may be good for rhubarb, but it's murder in the bloodstream.

My favourite rugby-injury story is beautifully short. It's about the referee who whistled up at a ruck and penalised a man for lying on the ball, only to find that he was completely unconscious. I like that. I don't expect to beat it, but I'm still looking.

A small but reassuring item of news

The least of Gordon Brown's injuries was the tooth extracted from his leg. The big Scottish lock had noticed a swelling, and when the doctor discovered an alien fang buried in the limb, Brown remembered colliding with another player in a recent club match. There is nothing extraordinary about the loss of a tooth; what is remarkable is that anyone had the strength to drive it so deep into the muscular shank of 'Broon from Troon'.

Years later, when Brown retired from rugby, he described all the other damage he had suffered, some of it self-inflicted. He had frequently aggravated his injuries by playing with pain-killing injections; and his right hand is now permanently weakened because he had been too impatient to let a broken bone mend properly. A player's career is short, especially at the very top, and Brown – like many others – often played with unhealed injuries rather than miss a game. 'I dread to think,' he wrote, 'what state I am going to be in by the time I reach the age of sixty. I know how many joints are currently bothering me at the tender age of thirty-five.'

The accepted wisdom among rowing men is that every University Boat Race docks five years from the lives of the oarsmen: all that sudden violent stress on the heart, you see; most unnatural. Between the wars, Rowe Harding said much the same of rugby: not good for the health:

> 'It is played above the natural pace of living and imposes a tremendous strain upon every organ in the body, and the weakest go to the wall . . . So many of the greatest exponents of Rugby have fallen into an early grave . . . One cannot but be struck by the large number of famous Rugby players who died untimely deaths . . .'

Cannot one? I turned to the records and prepared to be struck. The records that came to hand were of England international players from 1871 onwards, but it's reasonable to suppose that their mortality was very comparable with players from other countries.

143

The brisk and exhilarating truth is that Rowe Harding was wrong. Playing rugby for one's country does not shorten one's life; quite the reverse. Of course it's possible to find examples of men who didn't last the Biblical span: Nim Hall dead at forty-seven; Reg Higgins at forty-nine; Arthur Young (eighteen caps at scrum-half in the 1920s) a victim of pneumonia in India when he was only thirty-one; and saddest of all, Dick Stafford, the Bedford prop who played in all four England games in 1912 when he was only nineteen and who died of spinal cancer the same year. But these are exceptions that prove the rule.

The overwhelming majority of international players go on, if not for ever, at least for the best part of a good bit. Using the alphabetical listing of all players capped by England, I took the first one hundred who have died (not including those killed in action) and I calculated their average life span. It came to a shade under seventy years. Two had died in their thirties and seven in their forties, but thirty had reached their eighties and two lived past ninety.

One of the octogenarians was the great Len Corbett, a superb centre, capped eighteen times by England in the 1920s. He lived such a long and hearty life that when he turned eighty his friends decided it was pointless to wait until he was dead before holding a memorial dinner. So they invited him to be guest of honour at his own, slightly premature, memorial dinner, where he could hear and enjoy all the tributes to his splendid career. When you haven't got to go, that's the way not to go.